The Unstuck Leader

The Unstuck Leader

Getting Unstuck
Staying Unstuck

Judy Sims

For John

Contents

Introduction

It's perfectly normal to cry on airplanes. I'm sure I read that somewhere.[1] Something about being neither here nor there makes you philosophical and before you know it, you're having a big boo-hoo at thirty thousand feet. It can happen to anyone.

For a time in my life, I was on an airplane every other week. Toronto –> New York. New York –> Toronto. Back and forth as I attempted to build my budding e-commerce start-up into a tech giant. And I confess, I had momentary lapses of fortitude on more than one of those airplanes. Fortunately, I didn't make a big wailing spectacle of myself, but I certainly muffled more than a few sniffles and wiped the odd tear as I stared out the window.

You see, I was stuck. Really, really stuck. I'd been stuck before, as a magazine publisher, as a corporate VP and as an embattled COO, but this time was different. This time the stuckness seemed to seep into all aspects of my life. It was deeply personal. And I didn't have the first clue of what to do about it.

---

[1] Actually, I read it in *The Atlantic*, "Why We Cry on Planes", October 1, 2013.

Around this time, I remember having lunch with a friend who was himself a budding CEO (he's now a very successful CEO). I told him that I felt my inability to move my company forward was a monumental failure of character. It seemed I was lacking something. I didn't have what it took. He told me I was being too hard on myself and that I should have fun experimenting until I found what worked. In saying that, my friend displayed a quality I've come to recognize as absolutely necessary in all Unstuck Leaders – something I call *wateriness*. To be watery, is to focus not so much on outcomes, but rather to be committed to exploration. When a watery person hits a wall, they don't curse the wall, or blame themselves for the wall being there, they simply move in a different direction. It's not personal. It's an adventure.

In the end, I was able to move my company to an exit, though a small one and not exactly what I (and my investors) had been hoping for. Technically, I was now unstuck, but my fascination with stuckness stayed with me. That fascination only grew in subsequent years as I worked as a strategic consultant and later, as an executive coach. Time and time again, I saw profound stuckness in my clients. And, as I had been during my stuckness, they were mystified. And they were blaming themselves.

I began to wonder; if so many leaders are stuck, what does that mean for the people and organizations they lead, and what does it mean for society as a whole? The world is growing more complex, more challenging, and less predictable. How will these stuck leaders take us where we need to go?

The truth is, most stuck leaders are perfectly adequate. Some may have moments of greatness, some are just phoning it in, others are in way over their heads, some are bullies, and a few may even be malicious, but most, are fine. And fine is just not enough. In our current cultural and economic environment, fine is a failure of leadership.

And that ain't good.

There had to be a better way.

I suspected my watery CEO friend wasn't alone and that there were other leaders who had also figured out how to get and stay unstuck. And so, I began a quest to find as many Unstuck Leaders as I could, and to use their collective wisdom to build a leadership philosophy that would create more leaders like them.

My first step was to initiate the Unstuck Project. I put word out that I was looking to talk to leaders across all fields and seniority levels about their experiences with stuckness. Over the next year, 100 generous people from around the world gave me their time and shared their stories. Soon, a framework for the Unstuck Leader began to emerge.

In addition to my own research, the Unstuck Leader philosophy has been heavily influenced by Strategic Intervention (the tradition of coaching I practice), the Adult Lifecycle and Self-renewal Process as articulated by the late psychologist Frederic M. Hudson, as well as the work of Peter Senge, Otto Scharmer and Katrin Kaufer, who are among the leading voices in the field of System Leadership Theory.

Through this work, I learned that being an Unstuck Leader has nothing to do with job title, market cap, number of Instagram followers or any other outward measure. I found unstuck CEOs, unstuck sales executives, unstuck business owners, unstuck operations managers and even unstuck unemployed people.

Rather, the key to being an Unstuck Leader, is existing in what I call an *expansive state*. Leaders in this state are grounded in strong core values and purpose, yet also maintain an openness to people, ideas and experiences.

To achieve this state, the Unstuck Leader is extremely adept at managing their need for certainty (the need to feel safe and secure), and their need for significance (the need to feel important and in control). They also have highly developed values systems. They don't allow these values to be imposed upon them by outside forces, but rather do the inner work required to arrive at the qualities of character that are essential to their own intellectual, emotional and spiritual wellbeing. These core values become an internal guidance system from which they operate, make decisions, create and innovate.

This inner alignment is the basis of Authentic Power; not the kind of power that comes from job titles and org charts, but the kind that comes from a deep understanding of who we are and how we want to interact with the world around us. An authentically powerful leader prioritizes truth over comfort. They see the world for what it is, not what they want it to be. They seek the best answers, not the easiest or most convenient ones.

This is tough stuff.

For most of us, the first hint of stuckness is met by fear. This fear intensifies our stuckness and in turn, our stuckness further reinforces our fear. Down and down we spiral, deeper and deeper until we forget who we are and what we want to achieve. We enter the opposite of an expansive state. We enter a *contractive state*.

I confess that when I was a stuck start-up CEO, I was most definitely in a contractive state. I became increasingly risk averse. Rather than experiencing the thrill of building something new with an energized team, I gritted my teeth, withdrew deeper into myself, and became ever more rooted in my stuckness. I thought I was doing all the right things. I read the books, I did the networking, I took the advice of my investors. But the truth was, I was stuck because I couldn't see past my own fear. My fear of loss, my fear of less and my fear of never. And above all, my fear of not being enough. What a terrible place to lead from. I had completely given up my authentic power.

There are of course, degrees of stuckness, and mine was pretty extreme. But most of us are unhappy with our progress in at least one area of our lives. We might feel we've reached a plateau at work, or that our health isn't as robust as we'd like it to be, or perhaps a creative endeavour has become a slog. And over time, that stuckness becomes entrenched, we feel increasingly helpless and we begin to identify as being a stuck person. This makes getting unstuck all the more difficult.

Unstuck Leaders are no different from the rest of us. They get stuck all the time. The difference is, they don't let stuckness define them. For them, it's a part of life. Rather than beating themselves up over it, they work through it, often joyfully. That's because at their core, Unstuck Leaders know that true leadership is as much about who and how we are, as it is about what we do.

In other words, you can't become an Unstuck Leader until you become an unstuck human.

That's why, while most leadership books are focused on all the amazing things that great leaders do, this book focuses on *how to be the kind of person* who does all the amazing things that great leaders do. And in doing so, the question becomes not how are we going to get unstuck, but how are we going to use our lives? We've each been given an extraordinary gift; this conscious, self-aware life. How are we going to use our particular mix of traits and talents and understanding to benefit the world around us? What is our purpose?

This book is for all leaders, be they the manager of a small team, or the CEO of a Fortune 500 company. It's also for people who are not in an official leadership role, but who nonetheless affect and connect those around them for a greater good. Small or big, official or unofficial, the principles are the same. And so is the need. The world needs Unstuck Leaders.

There's an oft-used phrase in Strategic Intervention coaching: *Where focus goes, energy flows*. I'm asking you to give me your focus for the next 251 pages. Because I know there's a powerful, unstuck version of you that wants to emerge, and when it does, extraordinary things will become possible.

Ready? Let's do this. The world is waiting for you.

Chapter 1
WHY WE GET STUCK

THAT TIME I GOT PUNCHED IN THE FACE

Not too long ago, I was walking to the subway on my way to meet a client. As I passed through a doorway, a tall young man with an impossibly long wingspan passed through the other side. He was with three work colleagues and was telling a story and they were all laughing. Just as our paths crossed, he gesticulated wildly, flinging his hands out to his sides.

And he punched me in the face.

My sunglasses went flying, but not before digging into my cheek bone, leaving what would become a nasty red welt. I'd never been punched in the face before. Shocked, I leaned against the nearest wall and tried to compose myself, but damn if it didn't hurt. A small crowd gathered round, and the man stood before me, equally in shock and more than a little embarrassed. After all, he'd just punched a middle-aged woman in the face. And in front of his work colleagues to boot.

Tears stinging the corners of my eyes, I shooed him away, took a deep breath and continued on to the subway. When I got to my client's office twenty minutes later, I told her what to my rattled mind, was already becoming a funny anecdote. After all, how often can you launch a meeting with the words, "I just got punched in the face!"

And then she said something innocuous that turned out to be, for me, the most amazing thing.

"Jeez, kinda makes you wonder what the universe is trying to tell you, doesn't it?"

I don't actually believe the universe punches people in the face, but it did make me think. If the universe *could* punch me in the face, why would it? What's going on in my life that needs to change, stop, or grow? What am I avoiding?

It didn't take long to figure it out. I was avoiding beginning The Unstuck Project. It had been three months since I'd decided to interview 100 people about their experiences with being stuck. And I hadn't done a thing. Not an email, not a phone call, nothing.

I was stuck on my Unstuck Project.

Well ain't that a punch in the face?

I'd reached a comfortable plateau. I had a full roster of clients, I was feeling more and more competent as a coach, and after much career upheaval, things were finally beginning to feel easy. Why on earth would I want to put myself out there by starting something new and difficult?

So I didn't. Until I got punched in the face.

Perhaps what the universe was trying to tell me was that my old friends *fear* (the need for certainty) and *ego* (the need for significance) were in the driver's seat. What if no one wanted to be interviewed? What if the interviews failed to reveal anything interesting? What if I went through the whole process and wrote the book and no one read it?

It's a slippery slope.

I knew I had to act immediately or risk never beginning, much less completing The Unstuck Project. So, that afternoon, I sent out ten emails requesting interviews. And the following week, I sent out ten more. All in all, it took a year to finish the project. And I'll tell you what, it's been the most joyful and rewarding experience of my professional life.

EXERCISE:

Ask yourself, if you were to get punched in the face today, what would the universe be trying to tell you?

THE UNSTUCK PROJECT

If you want to be inspired and energized, ask a whole lot of people to tell you about their moments of greatest fear and triumph. As a part of The Unstuck Project, I did just that. I asked 100 people who are in my sphere, but whom I don't know well, if at all, to tell me about the times in their lives that they've felt the most stuck, the most frustrated and the most hopeless. Many of them went on to tell me about how they were able to work their way out of their stuckness. Others confessed they were still deep in the mud of it all and were unable to see a way out. Their openness, honesty, courage and resilience was humbling.

Toward the end of the project, I took joy in telling my subjects, which interview number they were – "You're number 87… 93… 99!" A few of them asked me if I was getting bored with the whole thing and my answer was always, "No". Everyone had an interesting story. Everyone had words of wisdom. In fact, often, an interviewee's stuckness related in some way to how I was feeling at that moment. More times than I can count, their words were exactly what I needed to hear.

My interviewees' stories and quotes will appear throughout this book, as illustrations of how stuckness happens, how it feels, and how it's possible to move forward. Their names will be changed, and their contributions will be lightly edited for clarity and/or brevity and to maintain anonymity.

After all those interviews, three things became very clear: stuck is pervasive, stuck is personal and most of all, stuck is perplexing.

Stuck is Pervasive

It wasn't difficult to find interview subjects for The Unstuck Project. Over 50 percent of the people I approached agreed to give me at least 30 minutes of their time. Perfect strangers volunteered through various Slack rooms and by filling out a form on my website. In turn, it wasn't difficult for my interviewees to land on an incident of stuckness to discuss. In fact, the biggest issue was choosing just one. Often, I was presented with a menu of stuck incidents to choose from. People were definitely into it.

Let's look at some stats.

I interviewed 45 women and 55 men in 35 cities in 12 countries.[2] Of the 100 interviewees, only 12 consider themselves to be "unsticky", in that they just don't get stuck. So, from this (admittedly unscientific) data, 88 percent of us experience stuckness at various points in our lives.

Just shy of one-third of my interviewees were CEOs, founders or general managers. People in top jobs were by far the most likely to respond to my interview request. It seems senior executives know a thing or two about the virtues of professional generosity and the benefits of networking. Head honchos also seem to be slightly less sticky than the rest of us – 19 percent of them claim to be unsticky as opposed to 12 percent of interviewees as a whole.

Most interviewees reported that they experience brief periods of stuckness that come and go throughout their lives. Except the creatives. They're stuck pretty much all the time.

---

[2] Yes, yes, I'm disappointed by the lack of gender balance too, but that's just the way the split happened.

> *"As a creative person, I'm in a perpetual state of stuckness. It's par for the course."*
>
> *– Max, Unstuck Project interviewee*

There were lots of types of stuckness, but by far, the most common was being in the wrong job (35 percent of interviewees), followed by being unable to move forward with a business project (17 percent), business issue (14 percent) or life stage (15 percent), and lastly, being unable to find the right "next thing" (7 percent).

We can get stuck at any age, though it seems most people experience their first incident of significant stuckness in their thirties. Of the interviewees who experienced a major incident of stuckness, the average age of its onset was 38. This is consistent with loads of academic research. The most quoted study, published in 2010 by the National Academy of Sciences reveals that a person's self-reported state of wellbeing drops beginning at age 38 and doesn't begin to improve until age 53 or so.[3] This is also consistent with a study by Happiness Works in the UK that found that people over 35 are twice as likely to be unhappy in their jobs as people under 35.[4] In case

---

[3] Arthur A. Stone, Joseph E. Schwartz, Joan E. Broderick and Angus Deaton, "A snapshot of the age distribution of psychological well-being in the United States", *PNAS*, June 1, 2010

[4] Will Martin, "Millennials are actually happy in their jobs – workers over 35, not so much", *Business Insider*, August 22, 2017

you're wondering, yup, this is what is sometimes referred to as the good-old midlife crisis.

So yeah, stuckness is pretty much everywhere. If you feel stuck, you're not alone. However, your particular form of stuckness is most definitely unique to you.

Stuck is Personal

What feels stuck to you might not feel stuck to me. We each have our own ideas of who we should be and how we should live our lives. And we each have our own needs, values and sense of purpose. If we're out of alignment with any of these things, we're going to feel stuck.

One thing I noticed over the course of the interviews is that when a person under 35 is feeling stuck, it's usually because they feel they're wasting time. They're in a rush to find the perfect job, in the perfect industry so they can get married and sign a mortgage and maybe have a baby or two. They're running hard to hit all their goals in life, and when they feel they're not doing that, the overwhelming emotions felt are frustration and impatience. Interviewee Zoey is a good example of this. Looking back on her moment of stuckness, she said, "I wasn't happy at work. I wasn't in a relationship. I was desperate to know what my life was going to be."

But for those over 35, the stuckness is more existential. It's about living a good life; a life with meaning and purpose. Interviewee Victoria was keen to leave her traditional job so that she could pursue a long-held entrepreneurial dream. As she put it, "I'm 58 and I'm not willing to do shit I don't like. There's going to have to be some joy in it."

What makes stuckness so personal is the meaning we attach to it. I, as an outside observer, might see your stuckness as merely a time of self-reflection or evolution. Or, I won't see it at all; I'll think you're kicking ass in the world. That's nice, but it doesn't matter to you. You feel stuck.

Interviewee Tristan has had what appears to be a highly challenging and rewarding career. But he doesn't feel that way. He has a lingering sense that he's not living up to his full potential. He told me, "I'm always feeling that what I'm doing should be bigger. I have a great life, but I feel like I should be doing more." Tristan, like many of us, is perplexed by his feelings of stuckness.

Stuck is Perplexing

When is stuck, stuck?

Rather than dealing with the negative emotions of stuckness, many of us refuse to see our stuckness for what it is.

In the best cases, this can lead to a positive reframing of the issue. People who reframe don't believe they're stuck, only that they haven't found the way forward yet. All twelve of the Unstuck Project interviewees who claimed to be unsticky use this form of reframing in their lives.

> *"I don't really think of difficult times as being stuck. You're in situations, there's things that you can control and things you can't control. You ask questions and face reality. And you do your best and there you go."*
>
> *– David, Unstuck Project interviewee*

Alternatively, refusing to acknowledge our stuckness can arise from a tricky form of denial. This happens when we delude ourselves into thinking we're not stuck because we're doing so much stuff.

Here's what that looks like:

- You can't quite get to the important items on your to-do list because you're so busy running around putting out small fires.

- Your code base/sales pitch/blog post is never quite good enough. It needs more revisions. You might even have to begin again from scratch.

- You feel you can't get going with that project until your desk is clean, and you've meditated, and you've lost twenty pounds.

- You can't launch that thing. It's not perfect yet.

- You don't want to talk about it.

The thing is, when your focus is on anything but your goal, you're not actually doing stuff. You're doing stuck.

There's always something keeping us from making that decision, moving forward with that project, or launching the thing that needs to be launched. If it seems your life is a never-ending series of small, annoying problems, you may want to look at where you're choosing to put your focus.

In my tradition of coaching, we call these types of problems, *Safe Problems*. Safe problems are distractions. What are they distracting us from? Well, *Quality Problems,* the kind of problems that when solved will launch us into a new life or business stage. Quality problems are hard. Really hard. But also, critical for us to feel fulfilled and for our careers and businesses to thrive.

As long as we're focused on safe problems, we can avoid dealing with the quality ones. We love to do this, because quality problems involve risk. They're things such as making a career change. Or deciding to go to marriage counseling. Or finally doing something about those sinking customer satisfaction scores, or lagging production times, or declining profitability trends.

We don't know if our quality problems are actually solvable. Or at least we don't know if we're up to solving them. And that's scary. So, we use safe problems to stay distracted, and ultimately, stuck. The perplexing thing is, we don't even know we're doing it.

Take interviewee Oliver. As he described his stuckness to me, he quoted several self-help books, mentioned a half-dozen conferences he'd been to, a couple of courses he'd taken, as well what his friends and family thought about his situation.

It became immediately obvious, that Oliver was doing stuck. And doing it very well, I might add.

Oliver had been very successful from a young age. After college, he'd moved from the east coast to California where he quickly rose to the top of his field. After several years of non-stop ninety-hour weeks, he was burnt out and fed up. To him, success had always meant fame and bigness and competitiveness. But those things no longer interested him. So rather courageously, he left California and moved home to begin something new. After a few missteps, he found himself at a crossroads.

"Small feels right. I love it. It feels disruptive. Where I'm challenged is that it's hard for me to visualize what small looks like for me."

Oliver wanted to follow his curiosity. He wanted to create. He didn't want to engage in crazy long work weeks or cut-throat competition. And he was fine with the potential consequences of that – what was (to some), a smaller life than he'd had in California. But there was a sticking point.

"I feel pressure to please people, and that's been a problem as I change my definition of success. I don't want to let people down. My whole life, everyone has understood or expected that I do interesting, great, and amazing things. And as I get older, that can be paralyzing."

Oliver wasn't in denial; he was well aware that he was stuck. The problem was that being stuck had become his safe problem. And all the books and conferences and courses and deep and meaningful conversations with his friends weren't going to solve it.

After some probing, Oliver was finally able to define the quality problem he'd been avoiding – how could he free himself from expectations and the need to be liked so he could move forward with a life and career that's aligned with his true self?

Or in his words, "Can small be great?"

Now he had something real to work on.

THE PATH TO STUCK

It All Starts with a Plateau.

Unless triggered by job loss, the death of a loved one, illness or some other form of externally imposed disruption to our lives, our stuckness is usually preceded by some kind of plateau. Either we've reached a new height of skill, experience and knowledge, or we're limited by circumstance or ability and we're unable or unwilling to move forward.

The plateau can be personal or professional in nature. Perhaps we've grown to despise the city we live in. Or we're no longer challenged in our job. Or we just can't hit an important business metric. Maybe we can't get that product launched or solve that staffing issue. For some reason, things have stopped moving forward as quickly as they used to.

Some people are perfectly cool with their plateau and can spend months, years or even decades swimming happily around in it, making small incremental changes, mentoring others, writing, speaking and sharing the skill and knowledge they've developed over time. I call them plateau swimmers. I love plateau swimmers. They're grounded in strong core values, they know themselves, and they know what they are and aren't willing to do. Yet, they maintain an open heart. They feel a vastness inside. They are, and are able to remain, in what I call a *healthy expansive state*. Warren Buffet is a plateau swimmer. So is Oprah Winfrey. And so was Mr. Rogers.

For most of us though, the plateau can bring about a sense of decline. You might call us plateau sinkers. Rather than finding joy in our new level of competence, we mourn the loss of the growth and excitement we experienced before the plateau.

"I had a feeling that maybe I had peaked. I was traveling around the world in business class. I had an amazing boss. But at the same time, I felt like I didn't know what leveling up to the next thing looked like. The kind of projects that helped me grow over the past four years started to look like stagnation. Roles above me looked like the same thing."

— *Amelia, Unstuck Project interviewee*

Getting stuck and unstuck is all about how we manage the plateau. A lack of introspection, as well as denial and avoidance can lead to limiting patterns of belief and behaviour that entrench us in our stuckness. We're out of alignment with our values and purpose. In this state, we're reacting to our world rather than creating it. This leads to feelings of powerlessness and even more stuckness.

The funny thing about plateaus is for most of us, they aren't immediately apparent. Looking back, several interviewees could see that they were stuck for months or even years before they realized it. It was a slow dawning.

Interviewee Parker knew he was miserable, but that was where his self-awareness ended. "I didn't know what it was. I wasn't looking introspectively enough at that pain point. I didn't stop to consider why I was getting so annoyed all the time."

Pauline, a mother and consultant who works from home actually had her realization during her unstuck interview. "I think I'm bored. It causes me to dread getting out of bed. I don't want to get up and make lunches and drop the kids at school. I'm bored of the routine. I'm bored of the grind."

Often, the slow dawning was capped by a revelatory ah-ha moment that helped interviewees finally acknowledge something was wrong. Greg, a consultant said, "I was on vacation with friends. We were talking about heading back to work on Monday and one of them said, 'I don't care about going back to work because my life only happens on the weekends.' I thought, *Oh how terrible, they've given their life to their company.* Then I realized I was in the same boat."

This is the point where non-plateau swimmers begin to sink. It's as if our life raft of complacency springs a leak and down we go, into a state of dissatisfaction, apathy and malaise. For some people, these feelings are a trigger to transition to a new life chapter. They might find a new job, launch a new initiative, shake up their working group or seek an internal department transfer. No longer at a plateau, they feel reenergized, challenged and focused. Until the next plateau, that is.

But some of us, mostly due to fear, resist transition. We grit our teeth and dig in. And when we do, the plateau becomes stuckness. Interviewee Abby let her fear keep her in a job she hated. "I had a lot of moments where I was like, *I'm going to quit right now*. And then someone would say something nice and I thought, *I can do it for a little longer.*"

Rather than initiating her own change, Tessa, an executive, held out hope that her employer would change. "I really wanted to do well for my boss. I wanted his approval. But that wasn't the kind of culture the company had. I spent too long trying to please a boss who didn't think in those terms."

The truth is, both Abby and Tessa admitted they were afraid to move on. And by staying where they were for too long, they were pulling themselves out of alignment with their core values.

Should over Could

When we live from a place of fear, we begin to prioritize values about who and how we *should* be over who and how we *could* be.[5]

Could values arise from our deepest truth and tend to be about things we want to experience, create or be. They're optimistic in nature. There are hundreds, if not thousands of *could* values such as curiosity, independence, integrity, love, honesty, joy, dignity, accountability, challenge and exploration. Each of us has our own unique combination of personally chosen *could* values, and usually, about three to five are core to who we are as people.

Should values on the other hand, are imposed upon us and are born of the things our parents and teachers might have said to us when we were young. We should be good boys or girls; we should not be too loud or outspoken. And then as we got a bit older, other people chimed in. We should be a certain weight, drive a certain kind of car, be a certain kind of son or daughter, spouse or parent. And yes, parenthood and particularly, motherhood, is the motherload of the *should* values. It seems a lot of people have a lot of thoughts about how we should raise our children, and even about our decision to have kids or not.

Once we're inculcated with a set of *should* values, we become our own enforcers. Zoey, a successful executive, believed she should be tough, unflappable and well, perfect. She became so good at enforcing her *should* values, when she found herself at a plateau, she felt guilt and

---

[5] Patrick Williams and Diane Menendez, *Becoming a Professional Life Coach, Lessons from the Institute for Life Coach Training*, 2007,217.

shame for not measuring up. "The pressure of wanting to be perfect and to do and say the right thing was paralyzing. I have a persona of a person who's cool and independent. But there was a crack in my armour. If someone saw the crack, it would have devastated me."

Should values are rampant at work where they tend to be about how we should act and what kind of employee we should be. *Should* values determine when to arrive at work and when to leave. What to wear and what not to. What's funny and what's not funny. When to speak up and when not to. When to debate and when not to. When to blow the whistle and when not to. A company's culture is largely formed of its collective *should* values. If you're unable to live up to a company's *should* values, you're unlikely to last in the job, no matter how well you perform. No wonder we prioritize *should* over *could*. The result though, is many of us finding ourselves doing things at work that are unlinked from our values, purpose and true selves.

"After two weeks on the job, I was told I'm too loud. And not very 'team-y'. And that really hurt me. I'd never heard that before. After that I was really careful. I didn't want to be the loud one or the one who doesn't fit in."

— *Abby, Unstuck Project interviewee*

The pressure to prioritise *should* over *could* happens at all levels of an organization. Everyone answers to someone. The CEO has a board and the board has shareholders and every one of them has thoughts on who we should be and how we should act.

Prioritizing *should* over *could* doesn't only happen at work. We can fall into the *should/could* trap in all areas of our lives, from our relationships to our creative endeavours to our personal goals and desires.

At work or at home, when we sacrifice what we *could* be for what we *should* be, we betray ourselves. And we know it. And that feels terrible.

This is when stuckness truly sets in.

Soon we fall into limiting patterns of belief and behavior that are both symptom and cause of our stuckness. We cling to certainty. We seek to bolster our egos. We may retreat into a La La Land of unrealistic expectations or succumb to the poison of cynicism. And all of this takes not only a mental toll, but also a physical one.

We are in what I call an *unhealthy contractive state*.

And if we're not careful, our stuckness can become entrenched.

The Trouble with Certainty

The need for certainty is a simple enough concept. We all want to feel safe and avoid pain. How could that possibly be a bad thing? Certainty makes us feel secure. It helps us sleep at night. It keeps our lives conflict free. When we're certain, no one can mess with us and nothing bad can ever happen.

Sounds wonderful!

Except, it's all an illusion.

In Buddhism, it's said that avoiding the unpleasant is what keeps us stuck. Preference for pleasure and avoidance of pain creates an imbalance. And in that imbalance, we shut ourselves off from our own potential. Because the opposite of certainty is curiosity. So, when we're certain, we're condemning ourselves to an incurious life.

How utterly boring.

And ultimately, how very unfulfilling.

Or as Pema Chodron (my favorite nun) puts it: "Change is just the way things are. If you're invested in security and certainty, you're not going to feel good a lot of the time."

Everyone has their own idea of what constitutes certainty. Some people feel secure living in a one-room apartment with a social security check. Others need a few million in the bank. And most of us fall somewhere in between.

Of course, there are positive ways to meet your need for certainty. For example, you can be financially responsible, putting away a portion of your paycheck each month to prepare for retirement. But, there's also a lot of negative ways. You can increase your income by moving to a new company, or you can stay stuck in a job you hate for years and years because you're afraid of change and challenge. You can prepare for the emerging future by continuing your education, or you can grasp back into the past, hunker down, and demand that the world around you just stop changing.

Certainty is tricky. It comes from the part of our brain that's waiting for a cougar to leap out of the forest at any moment. The problem is, because it's not very advanced, it doesn't know the difference between the danger of a cougar and that of a nerve-wracking business presentation. It perceives the risk of both with the same intensity. So, we end up living a lot of our lives in a state of fear that isn't real.

In her book, *Big Magic*, writer Elizabeth Gilbert describes this kind of fear as, "…a mall cop who thinks he's a Navy SEAL: He hasn't slept in days, he's all hopped up on Red Bull, and he's liable to shoot at his own shadow in an absurd effort to keep everyone 'safe'."

Why would anyone listen to that guy?

Let's have a closer look. (Pictures of brains are gross, so I traced one and made it fun and stripy rather than grey and slimy. You're welcome.)

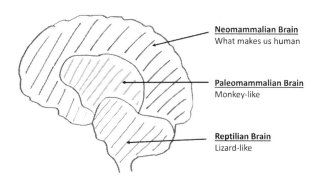

EVOLUTIONARY STAGES OF BRAIN DEVELOPMENT

What you see presented in the figure above are the three evolutionary stages of our brain's development.

The deepest part of our brain is reptilian. It's lizard-like. And it has all the personality of a lizard, i.e., none. We need it to survive, but mostly it's concerned with keeping the lights on. It's busy with things such as breathing and elimination. Our lizard brain often gets blamed for our fearful emotions, but he's not the primary culprit.

The real trouble maker is the limbic system, or paleomammalian brain. It's on the lookout for cougars. It's all about survival. And, it's where our emotions reside. So, in our brains, emotions are tied to survival. When we're feeling frozen in fear or blinded by anger, it's our limbic system that's in charge. The paleomammalian brain is often described as Monkey-like. You may have heard people who are into meditation talk about their monkey brain or how they need to tame their monkey brain. This is the part of the brain they're talking about. I'll get back to the monkey in a moment.

Finally, we have the outermost, or neomammalian part of our brain. It was the most recent part to evolve. It's where our personality develops, it's where we do our thinking, and it's responsible for language. It's the part of our brain that makes us human. It likes to create and solve problems.

Unfortunately, our trouble-making monkey brain is a powerful thing. It's very loud. And a lot of the time, it's very afraid. It likes to tell us over and over again how scared it is, and how terrible the world is, and how if we're not careful, awful, awful things will befall us. And because of this, it craves certainty. And so do we.

We absolutely, positively, positively MUST learn to tame our monkey brain and make friends with uncertainty.

Why?

Because when you look at the brain, you see that a good chunk of it (the reptilian brain and paleomammalian brain) is occupied with survival and not truth.[6]

So here's some truth.

Our tolerance for uncertainty is directly related to the quality of our lives. The less certainty we need, and the more comfortable we are with uncertainty, the less we will listen to our monkey brains and the more fulfilled we'll be.

Or as Eckhart Tolle puts it, "When you become comfortable with uncertainty, infinite possibilities open up in your life."

The Problem with Ego

The first thing you need to know about your ego is that it's not you. It's a structure built of a lifetime of experience, disappointment and pain (and some good stuff too). Your true self is the consciousness that lies beneath the ego. It's built of love and purpose. But your ego doesn't want you to know that. That trick of the ego is that it convinces you that it is you.

Ego arises from our need for significance. Just as our need for certainty isn't inherently bad, neither is our need for significance. Having a high need for it doesn't automatically make you a malignant narcissist. Significance is another way of saying that we need to feel

---

[6] If you want to learn even more about the brain, hop on over to WaitButWhy.com where blogger Tim Urban does a phenomenal job explaining its quirks and mysteries. His post called "Neuralink and the Brain's Magical Future", from April 20, 2017, is a masterpiece and it very much inspired the brain discussion in this book.

that we matter. We need to be validated. That's just human. And it's universal. But, if we don't manage it well, our need for significance can develop into a significant problem.

When we operate from a mismanaged ego, the world is about me, me, me rather than we, we, we. This limits our field of view, and the resulting tunnel vision can have a severe impact not only on our personal fulfillment in life, but also on our ability to be effective leaders and contributors.

Leaders with a high need for significance believe that they have all the answers. And because of this, they fail to reach out to others for information and feedback. Bad ideas aren't quashed, and great ideas aren't heard. Rather than learning from the success of others, they become threatened by it or resentful of it. This leads to more isolation and more tunnel vision. More me, me, me.

When our need for significance takes prominence, nothing is ever enough. If we have a million dollars, we want ten million. If the audience applauds loudly, we want a standing ovation. This perpetuates feelings of stuckness, because we're never satisfied. A high need for significance can lead to pointless competitiveness that is detached from our *core* values. We need the biggest house on the block, the nicest car, the hottest spouse. With each win, we take ourselves further away from who we really are. We become slaves to our own images and purchases.

The result? Stuck. Stuck. Stuck.

Sam, a CTO at a medium-sized technology company, worked for months on a new product strategy. True to his ego-driven self, he did all the work alone, including market research, product design, sales strategy and pricing. When Sam presented his recommendation to the company's executive team, there were serious concerns and the CEO declined to move forward with the plan.

A week later, during our coaching session, Sam was beside himself "My CEO didn't even see all the work I'd put into the strategy! It's obvious this is the direction in which we need to take the company, why is he being so blind?" I asked Sam why he thought his boss rejected his proposal. He gave several answers.

"Because he hates me."

"He doesn't understand me."

"He's mad at me."

"He's threatened by me."

Me. Me. Me. All Sam's answers came from his ego. He didn't attempt to put himself in the CEO's shoes. He didn't consider alternate perspectives. And, he dismissed the feedback he was given during the presentation.

The truth was, Sam's proposal, though very clever, also included a lot of risk. If not executed properly, there was a good chance it would disrupt the company's core revenue stream.

Sam knew this. But he just couldn't see past himself and his idea. Had he considered the CEO's perspective, as well as those of his colleagues, he might have framed his recommendations differently. They might have had a productive conversation about how they could implement Sam's plan while protecting existing revenues.

When people operating from ego are faced with confrontation or disagreement, they become defensive (He hates me!) rather than introspective (How could I have framed my arguments differently?). Their egos won't let them accept responsibility. Rather, they place blame elsewhere, never learning from their mistakes, thus condemning themselves to repeat them.

Now that's stuck.

I'm sure you're wondering if I was able to coach Sam to a less ego-driven perspective. Nope. I wasn't. You can't win them all. But, he's since moved on to a new organization where I believe he's much happier.
Sometimes, the ego flares because we're in in a job or place that's just not for us. And once we find a better fit, it quiets down again.

The Downside of the Upside

Optimism is good. Everyone knows that. Optimism sets the stage for success by giving us the fortification we need to stick with it through the good and the bad. An optimistic perspective is good for both our physical and metaphorical hearts, because optimistic people are more likely to lead a healthy lifestyle and reach out to friends and family for support.[7]

However…

There's a difference between optimism and La La Land.

When we dream about all the amazing things we want to do with our lives and imagine exactly how good it will feel when we reach our goals and then bask in the joy of all that wonderful future-state happiness, we're not actually doing ourselves any favors. In fact, that La La Land

---

[7] Ciro Conversano, Alessandro Rotondo, et al, "Optimism and Its Impact on Mental and Physical Well-Being", *Clinical Practice and Epidemiology in Mental Health*, 2010

dreaming could be keeping us from achieving what we want.

It turns out, optimism is a complicated thing. And contrary to almost everything you've heard and read, rather than fuel our determination, an excess of optimism can actually hold us back.

You: Whaaaaat?

Me: Let's start with the basics.

Each of us has three minds: the negative, the positive and the neutral.

We all know the certainty-loving negative mind to be a bad thing. But sometimes, it gets a bad rap. The negative mind is our protector. It signals potential danger and harm. It's beautiful.

But when we exist too much in the negative mind, we can become reactive. That is, we expect things to go poorly, people to let us down, and life to be difficult; and we react accordingly. And, we get stuck.

Okay. No surprises so far.

Now let's look at the positive mind. This is where excitement and enthusiasm are born. Those are good things. But there's a difference between a disposition that allows us to believe that things will generally work out and drifting off to a La La Land of fantasies and outlandish expectations. Is it truly realistic to expect our start-up to be worth a billion dollars in two years? Or to expect a new life partner to solve all our problems? Or to believe we can lose those twenty pounds in three weeks, just in time for our high school reunion?

When we go to La La Land, it's usually because there's a fear or need that we're afraid to look at. And this pulls us away from who we are. In fact, it causes us to disrespect who we are. And when things don't work out, all the worries and fears we dismissed come back in a tsunami of negative emotions. And you know how that turns out. Yup, stuck.

What are the fears the overly positive mind refuses to look at? The big three are fear of loss, fear of less and fear of never.

We might fear we'll lose our:

- Job
- Partner
- Friends
- Self-respect

We might fear we'll have less:

- Money
- Happiness
- Time
- Love

We may fear we'll never:

- Be rich
- Be thin
- Be loved
- Feel good about ourselves

At their core, the big three fears are really about the fear of not being enough. And if we're not enough, then perhaps, we're not loveable. And that thought is unbearable. So, we ignore it. And we push ourselves into the positive. And if we're not careful, we end up in La La Land.

La La Land isn't a very productive place. In her book, *Rethinking Positive Thinking*, Gabriele Oettingen writes that "The pleasurable act of dreaming seems to let us fulfill our wishes in our minds, sapping our energy to perform the hard work of meeting the challenges in real life."

A far better place to be is the neutral mind. The purpose of the neutral mind is to weigh information. There, we can listen and observe without judgement. We can create without fear or ego. And, we can learn from our mistakes without self-recrimination. In the neutral mind, we have clarity.

Think of it this way. The negative and positive minds are where stories live. (This is awesome/this is terrible. I'm a genius/I'm a fraud.) They're about reacting. And they drain our energy.

The neutral mind is where intuition lives. It sees the world as it truly is. It sees us as we truly are. It's about responding. And this builds our energy.

The Poison of Cynicism

In the novel *The Bonfire of the Vanities*, author Tom Wolfe refers to cynicism as a "cowardly form of superiority."

Sounds harsh? I don't think so.

Cynicism is a poison that seems to have found its way into our collective hearts. It used to be that my generation,

Generation X, was known for its cynicism, but I have to hand it to the Millennials – they seem to have outdone us.

I suspect the specifics of this age of cynicism, and why it seems to have infected the Millennial generation with such force will be the topic of many future Ph.D. theses. Maybe it's a result of being raised on *The Simpsons* and *The Office*, or maybe it's due to meme culture, or having come of age during the great recession of 2008, or the crushing pressure of student debt, or the unaffordability of even the tiniest studio apartment. These all seem like reasonable explanations, but they don't make the resulting cynicism any less poisonous.

Psychologist Frederic Hudson calls cynicism a "failure of nerve" and he credits it as one of the most prevalent reasons we become stuck, particularly in midlife. In his book *The Adult Years, Mastering the Art of Self-Renewal*, Hudson states that "Motivation to make life work is disabled by a vicious circle: personal daring and adult empowerment are curtailed by social disillusionment and cynicism; social empowerment is curtailed by reduced personal vision, motivation and leadership."

Do you get it?

Millennial or not, we must diligently watch for cynicism in ourselves. Because it's impossible to create, innovate, and to find joy and fulfillment in life if we indulge in the cowardly superiority, and the failure of nerve, that is cynicism.

Because what cynicism tells us is that nothing matters. There's no point in trying, and in fact, it's stupid to try. Only fools try.

Unstuck Project interviewee Felix was an executive at a consulting firm, when the company was acquired by a competitor. Felix was flattered when he was asked to sign a retention agreement. That is, he agreed that he would stay with the company for at least a year to help with the transition to new ownership, and in return, he'd be awarded a substantial cash bonus.

It sounded great on paper, but it didn't take long before Felix felt terribly stuck.

"It was incredibly unpleasant. They came in, took over everything I had worked for and everything I thought was important, and then said, 'No thanks, none of this is valuable to us.' It was a huge, wild disconnect. Like watching someone wear your clothes."

As Felix's stuckness grew, so did his cynicism. "There was a realization that I was on the losing team. Nothing was working. I wasn't motivated to get things done. I tried to divorce myself from it and just collect a paycheck until I could receive my retention bonus."

Felix believed he was "on the losing team". That's where cynicism is truly born. I'm on the losing team, so I no longer care. The whole game is stupid. I'm better than the game. The game is for suckers.

Felix fell into the cynicism trap. "I used to say, 'Not my monkey. Not my circus.' My wife and I used to joke about it. But I came to realize, it also robbed me of my agency."

And that's the point. Cynicism is poison because it paralyzes us. It prevents us from acting in our own best interest. And, it makes us feel oddly superior at the same time. It's like scratching an itch, but it leaves a gaping wound. It doesn't make us smarter. It doesn't protect us from pain. It only gives us a false sense of certainty and the kind of significance that leaves us empty. Do not give in to it.

Felix saw his cynicism for the poison it was, gathered his courage and recovered his agency. He left the company, leaving his retention bonus on the table. The money didn't matter. Felix needed to break his unhealthy pattern and get back into alignment, so he could move on with his life.

If you want to end your cynicism – and you have to if you want to achieve anything worthwhile in life – then you must allow yourself to be vulnerable. And that takes courage. You might look stupid. You might fail. You might get hurt. Felix walked away from a high five-figure bonus. That took guts. But to him, it was a small price to pay for his integrity.

And that's why Felix is no longer stuck.

The Physical Toll of Stuckness

About six months into my stint as the Vice President of Digital Media at a large newspaper company, my face exploded.

Why? Because I was stuck.

Being the VP Digital at that particular newspaper company, at that particular time was a mighty tough gig. I had had a bad feeling about the role, but I took it anyway, blinded by money and status. After all, I was the youngest female VP in the company's history. Woopty doo!

Inevitably, I hit a wall that I couldn't push through. And soon, my face broke out in severe cystic acne. I was in my late thirties, an executive responsible for millions of dollars of revenue per year, and I was covered in zits. At its worst, I counted thirteen giant cysts on my chin, forehead and cheeks. My stuckness was written all over my face. It still is. That terrible time has left me with physical scars.

Our bodies are often the first place that stuckness manifests. Unstuck Project interviewee Tessa has a theory that I agree with. She says, "When you're not authentically yourself, it impacts your health. Your body will let it out because you're too much of a professional to let it show in your emotions." Amen sister.

According to the American Psychological Association, stress can affect your musculoskeletal system leading to migraines, pinched nerves and other unpleasant conditions.[8]

Penelope, another Unstuck Project interviewee, was bullied by her boss. Nothing she could do was right. She was belittled on a regular basis and there were constant battles. Despite the bullying, Penelope deeply respected and admired her boss. So, she began to internalize the bullying. And she began to believe that she was unworthy. This rendered her less and less effective in her job. She was stuck. And the physical toll of those weeks and months was substantial. "I carry a lot of my stress and anxiety in my neck and shoulders. I developed double vision in my left eye. My left shoulder was literally up to my ear. I had a lot of tests, but it was a massage therapist who ultimately fixed it."

Sophia, a company director, experienced back pain to the point where she couldn't walk. "There was a compressed nerve in my back that caused me to lose function in my right foot."

---

[8] http://www.apa.org/helpcenter/stress-body.aspx

The physical toll of stuckness isn't just a female thing. The men I interviewed reported crippling back pain, sleep disorders, migraines, an increase in drinking and a decrease in exercise during their stuck moments.

Chronic stress causes our bodies to remain on guard all the time, as if waiting for Freddy Krueger to burst into our living room. When we're unable to release that tension, trouble ensues.

Stress also stimulates the release of the hormone cortisol, which can affect the functioning of both the male and female reproductive systems and leave one drained of energy. An abundance of stress-induced cortisol caused Unstuck Project interviewee Mia, a CEO, to suffer a terrible hormonal imbalance that left her in bed for two years. But that didn't stop her, she ran her company from her bed, creating more stress, and prolonging her illness.

The stress of stuckness can affect the cardiovascular, gastrointestinal and respiratory systems in a multitude of ways, from heart problems to stomach troubles to asthma attacks.

But perhaps the scariest stress-effect is how it can age us prematurely by shortening our telomeres, the sections of our DNA that live at the ends of chromosomes.[9] Their job is to keep our chromosomes from unravelling. Trust me, you don't want unravelling chromosomes – they can lead to Parkinson's, Type 2 Diabetes, cardiovascular disease and cancer.

According to researchers, what we eat and how much we exercise influences the length of our telomeres.[10] I

---

[9] https://www.huffingtonpost.ca/entry/stress-aging-process_n_3047000

[10] https://ideas.ted.com/could-your-thoughts-make-you-age-faster/

suppose that's not too surprising. But how about this: negative thought patterns such as cynical hostility, pessimism, rumination, suppression and mind wandering (going off to La La Land) shorten the length of our telomeres.

That's right – your telomeres are listening to all your negative shit. And they're reacting accordingly.

Chances are, if you're unravelling, so are your chromosomes.

Okay. Have I scared you enough?

Good.

In my practice, I cheer when a client tells me they're stuck. Suddenly, they don't have all the answers. And that means there's an opening. They're ready for something new.

A new chapter.

"Life is about being stuck. Without stuckness, we never gain traction."

— *Kyle, CEO*

Chapter 2
A NEW KIND OF LEADER

Meet Bob. He's a CEO.

Bob's a vision guy. He believes his personal brand of visionary leadership is imperative to his company's continued health and success. He is fiercely loyal to and protective of his team and has fostered an "us against the world" mentality when dealing with suppliers, regulators and sometimes, even customers. He's a great problem solver who reacts quickly and decisively during a crisis, and there are lots of crises to react to. Though he has set targets, created a clear reporting structure and put operating policies and procedures in place, he often handles things on his own because he doesn't want his team to know that at times, the company has been in danger of going under. He gives great, constructive feedback at annual reviews. He's a relentless competitor who is deeply focused on driving his target numbers each and every quarter. But, he's also a fact-based decision maker and loves a good debate. He has his go-to data people who know exactly the kind of information he likes and needs when making decisions. And to keep himself motivated, he seeks out life-hacking books, videos and articles. And even though the company has stalled and maybe even begun to backslide in the past few months, Bob won't give up. He'll keep fighting.

Bob seems to have the qualities most of us believe make for a good leader. But the truth is, Bob is stuck. And that's because as diligent and focused as he is, he's bought into an outdated leadership mythology.

THE THREE MOST DAMAGING LIES WE TELL OURSELVES ABOUT LEADERSHIP

Most of the leadership mythology we subscribe to was created in the 20th century world of fossil fuels and mechanistic, production-oriented businesses. In the 21st century, that world is dying. We can see before us a new world, one of ideas, knowledge and innovation, but we're not quite there yet. It's still emerging. And as a result, we're kind of in between things.

Stepping into a new leadership philosophy is a slow process. And it's messy. In the old era, leadership was about efficiency and uniformity, and the best way to achieve that was highly structured, top-down direction. But in a world where everything is changing, top-down can no longer work. Or as Otto Scharmer and Katrin

Kaufer put it in their book, *Leading from the Emerging Future*, "Our inherited leadership vocabulary is no longer fit to meet the challenges of our time."

On some level, we all sense the need for a new leadership vocabulary. But first, we must break free of the lies that keep us from re-examining just what a leader is and should be.

Lie 1: Leaders are Either Heroes or Scapegoats

It's difficult not to romanticize the heroics of leaders of spectacularly successful companies. They had a gloriously ambitious vision (or several visions in the case of Elon Musk) and they made it a reality. They were tested and persevered through extreme adversity and yet, they prevailed.

But these leaders are also human (thank god) and as such, they're also (sometimes deeply) flawed. And if and when they ultimately fail, each of them will become a scapegoat. They couldn't cut it. They weren't strong enough. You're good or you're bad. You're in or you're out. A winner or a loser. It's personal. And frankly, childish.

The problem with the leader as the be-all-end-all hero-visionary-superstar is that it assumes the people who work for those leaders are feckless followers who are in need of someone to tell them what to do and how to do it. In his book, *The Fifth Discipline*, Peter Senge wrote, "At its heart, the traditional view of leadership is based on assumptions of people's powerlessness, their lack of personal vision and inability to master the forces of change, deficits which can only be remedied by a few great leaders."

This is not the way to create an organization that can adapt and thrive in uncertain times. It is the way though, to create employees who are cynical, or worse, unwilling to take risk and responsibility at work.

It's a great way to get stuck.

Unstuck Leaders are not heroes, they're mortal. It's time we all got over this hero thing.

Lie 2: Leaders Create Organizational Order

We believe that leaders should set the goals for a company and then implement policies and procedures to accomplish those goals. Company standards, regulations, workflows, performance metrics, etc. are all designed as top-down mechanisms of control. We believe that leaders are the best qualified to arrive at optimal solutions for organizational problems.

The real world just doesn't work that way. There are multiple informal systems in place in any organization that actually get the work done. Floor employees and supervisors have their own hacks and methodologies that senior management has no knowledge of. There are also informal networks of communication, favor trading and resource sharing all happening under senior management's radar. Employees often ignore organizational charts and regulations. They self-organize in spite of them. They break the rules. They create workarounds. And, they get shit done.

To try to impose order on these complex adaptive behaviors would be madness. And ill-advised to boot. Creative solutions arise out of tension, not order. When rules are enforced with an iron fist, innovation dies. Weak leaders create a false sense of security out of order and it gets them stuck.

Unstuck Leaders understand that informal systems are forming without them. They learn to understand them and then empower the teams and employees within them to do their thing. Notice that I didn't say "harness" them. That's not what this is about. The challenge for the Unstuck Leader is to not take control, but rather enable.

The thought of giving up control makes many leaders feel nauseous. That's why Unstuck Leaders are so rare.

Lie 3: Leaders Provide Certainty in Times of Uncertainty

Most of us are not fans of uncertainty. Not a lot of people would say, "Yes please, bring me a whopping helping of I-don't-know-what's-going-to-happen!".

That's why, during times of uncertainty, we like nothing more than a strong leader to take charge. We like it even better if said leader can also reassure us that he or she will stop the change, put an end to uncertainty and restore the past as it was. Even better still, we'd like to be assured that things aren't really that complicated, that they are in fact simple and the old ways of doing things will continue to work once we just get past this one little blip.

This type of denial is what's known in Systems Leadership Theory as "absencing".

Rather than bravely stepping into the future, we cling to the past. We shut ourselves off from what is emerging. We turn our backs on those being affected by the change and ultimately, we turn our backs on ourselves. We're left incapable of responding and creating and innovating. When we live in an absencing cycle, we're betraying ourselves. It's the ultimate self-own.

Scharmer and Kaufer believe this pattern of reaching into the past creates stuckness by limiting the organization to a single ideology (one way), an "us vs. them" mentality (othering) and perhaps most troublingly, a single will (fanaticism).

You only need look to the current state of American politics to see absencing in practice. The irony of absencing is that it can look like strong leadership, but it is in fact, an abdication of leadership. When we're certain, we don't seek out uncomfortable facts and data. We don't seek out opposing views. And we're left unprepared to face the challenges of the rapidly changing world we're attempting to deny.

The Unstuck Leader understands that leadership is about accepting uncertainty and ambiguity and learning to thrive despite them. An Unstuck Leader's job is to give employees certainty within the uncertainty. And that doesn't mean telling them lies, nice stories or giving them false confidence and reassurance. It means giving them the only kind of certainty that matters. The certainty of co-created values, purpose, mission and vision. And it means showing them how to cultivate those things within themselves as well as within the organization.

Ultimately, Unstuck Leadership is about prioritizing truth over comfort. And that's why we have to let go of the lies. It's time to step out of the old, and into what's emerging.

Meet Chris. He's also a CEO.

Chris too, is a vision guy.[11] He engages his team in an ongoing process of co-creation where the vision is repeatedly evaluated and adjusted to meet the changing marketplace. Chris and his team include their suppliers, regulators, customers and community in their long-term vision. Team members are encouraged to work within their personal values systems as well as that of the organization. This personal alignment frees employees to fully express their creativity, producing better solutions to problems they encounter. Because Chris and his team are so connected to the systems in which the company operates, they're able to sense what's emerging in their industry and community. This allows them to anticipate difficulties and develop strategies before they become crises. Chris is devoted to enabling his team to do their best work and sees his primary role as that of the "obstacle remover". Chris doesn't do annual reviews. He prefers a continuous feedback cycle, both giving and receiving accolades and constructive criticism. While Chris understands that he must be competitive in the marketplace, he's also focused on the long-term growth and health of the company, rather than one quarter at time.

---

[11] Note: I chose to make both Bob and Chris male in this example because I didn't want so-called "gender norms" to affect the perception of what makes an Unstuck Leader and what makes a stuck leader. All genders have the capacity to be stuck and unstuck.

Chris loves facts and debate, but only within the larger context of the systems at play inside and outside of his organization. When making decisions, he resists going to the same people for the same data, over and over. Rather, he seeks out a variety of sources and perspectives. He likes to experiment, and then use his learnings from those experiments to do things better the next time around. And to keep himself motivated, Chris ensures that he's living up to his values and purpose each and every day. His company is growing, staff engagement is high, and productivity and profitability are increasing.

Chris is most certainly unstuck.

And that's because Chris understands the nature of complexity.

UNSTUCK LEADERS ENABLE COMPLEX ADAPTIVE SYSTEMS

You already know what complex adaptive systems are, even if you don't know you know. You've seen them in practice. You've watched teams self-organize to address a problem. You've watched cross-functional interactions resulting in product or service changes. You've watched companies adapt to new situations or environments.

Complex adaptive systems form, learn, shift, adapt, disintegrate and regenerate. And it's constant. It emerges out of the very nature of an organization – the connection of disparate parts that are bonded by a common goal or need. Kind of like a neural network, there are multiple nodes connecting to multiple other nodes in multitudes of ways. The stimuli, such as market conditions, interpersonal relationships, serendipitous discoveries, product failings, competitor actions, customer feedback, supplier changes, or government regulation, cause tension, which results in creative solution finding.

The process is inevitable. It cannot be codified, it cannot be regulated, and it cannot be stopped. It's really about the stuff that happens every day as people are doing their jobs. The best a leader can hope for is to understand the systems that affect the organization and based on this understanding, seek to enable them, influence them and/or, adapt to them.

Here's the way scholars like to talk about complex adaptive systems:

"Using the concept of complex adaptive systems, we propose that leadership should be seen not only as position and authority but also as an *emergent, interactive dynamic* – a complex interplay from which a collective impetus for action and change emerges when heterogeneous agents interact in networks in ways that produce new patterns of behaviour or new modes of operating."[12]

A bit dry don't you think?

Maybe a story will help.

COMPLEXCORP

Tracy is the head of logistics at ComplexCorp. One day, she gets a call from Khaled, the company's head of

---

[12] Mary Uhl-Bien, Russ Marion, Bill McKelvey, *Complexity Leadership Theory: Shifting leadership from the industrial age to the knowledge era*, 2007, 299.

production. Khaled tells Tracy that Supplier X's last shipment was ten percent light and that she should watch to ensure they're invoiced appropriately.

Tracy checks with accounts payable and not only has Supplier X billed the full amount for the shipment, they've asked for fifteen-day payment rather than the usual thirty days. Tracy calls her Supplier X sales rep to find out what's going on, only to be told that he's left the company.

Tracy decides to visit Mary, who heads up the legal department to get a read on her options. Mary mentions that she heard a rumour just that morning that new industry regulations will soon force Supplier X to make significant changes to their product, or risk substantial penalties.

Mary makes some calls to a few of her government contacts and confirms that new industry regulations are on the way.

Tracy and Khaled do some research and discover that Supplier Z, a new Supplier X competitor, is already compliant with the new government regulations.

Mary agrees to rush through an RFP, circumventing the company's usual process. Within a month, the company has contracted Supplier Z which not only provides better quality but is less expensive. Unlike other clients of Supplier X, production at ComplexCorp is not interrupted, giving the company a massive competitive advantage resulting in a ten percent increase in sales.

No one asked Tracy, Khaled and Mary to find a new supplier. No taskforce was created to determine a way to

increase revenue by ten percent; nor would Tracy, Khaled
or Mary have been assigned to that taskforce if it had been
created. Rather, ComplexCorp's leaders created a culture
that enabled the behaviour that led to the discovery of
Supplier X's impending difficulties. The rest, just kind of
happened. In complex leadership theory, this process is
called *Emergence*. And it's everything.

The formal definition of Emergence is: a non-linear
change in a complex system. In practice, that means
something happens not because of the top-down structure
of an organization, but because of the interconnectedness
of people and systems inside and outside of the
organization. An organization that values the power of
emergence is more competitive, faster moving, more
creative and dynamic and its employees are more
engaged, passionate and loyal. Leaders who value
emergence tend to operate from an *eco-system* perspective
rather than an *ego-system* perspective.

What does that mean?

Let's go back to Bob and Chris.

Bob is operating from an ego-system. He's prioritizing
his needs for certainty and significance. And as such, he's
focused on himself, his immediate team, hierarchy,
personal achievement and short-term timelines. He's
independent and decisive. This allows him to meet his
quarterly numbers most of the time. But, his lack of focus
on the world around him, and his need to be the
company's primary problem solver leaves him blind to
what is emerging and therefore, less prepared for the
future.

Chris is operating from an eco-system. He's prioritizing
his needs for growth and contribution. As such, he's

focused on the networked independence of himself and his team within the eco-system in which his company operates. He thinks long-term. He is open, communicative and transparent. He gives permission for his team to be the same way. This makes it easier for them to sense what's emerging in the world and to be successful within it.

Basically, it's me, me, me (ego) vs. we, we, we (eco).

The complexity of operating from an eco-system makes it much more difficult than operating from the relative simplicity of an ego-system. But despite its challenges, the eco-system is a far better reflection of the times we're in. The world is complex. The world is connected. To ignore this is to turn a blind eye to reality.

HOW TO TELL A STUCK LEADER FROM AN UNSTUCK LEADER

A Stuck Leader is Certain.
An Unstuck Leader is Watery.

A stuck leader is tied to the past. Their need for certainty causes them to deny the future that is emerging around them. And frankly, they're denying themselves, or rather their true selves as well. They're out of alignment. A symptom of this misalignment is when a leader prioritizes *should* values over *could* values. That is, they focus on what they should do and be, over what they could do and be.

Should is limiting. Options are narrowed. Possibilities are stunted.

Should is a product of fear. And fear leads to entrenchment. There's only one reality. There's us and there's them. And there's only one right way for things to be done. For a leader with a high need for certainty and significance, this entrenchment feels safe and comfortable. But in reality, it's anything but. It puts them in a contractive state. It makes them small. And over time, completely ineffective.

An Unstuck Leader is watery. They're listening and watching for what's emerging around them. They're tuned into the story, the trend, or the shift in the collective consciousness that will change everything. For them, it's all about *could* values. They focus on what they and their organization could be or do.

That said, watery Unstuck Leaders aren't attached to a particular outcome or circumstance. They have an idea of where they'd like to go and they are committed to a healthy and growing bottom line, but they aren't locked into a set of steps to get there.

They don't have to have all the answers. But they do have to be curious and observant. They have to ask tons of questions. And they can't be afraid to ask seemingly stupid or obvious ones. This is how employees know that everything is up for examination and change.

The Unstuck Leader's watery quality is enabled by their mastery of the self-renewal process. Upon hitting a plateau in life or business, they don't allow themselves to become discouraged and demotivated. Rather, they make use of the skills they've acquired. They engage deeper. They transition to new places, new cultures and new areas of focus.

An Unstuck Leader is in alignment with their personal values, purpose and mission. They are action oriented. They are committed and consistent. They have strong core values and an open heart. They're expansive in nature.

In her book *Mindset, The New Psychology of Success*, Carol Dweck perfectly defines the difference between certainty and wateriness.

"In one world – the world of fixed traits – success is about proving you're smart or talented. Validating yourself. In the other world – the world of changing qualities – it's about stretching yourself to learn something new. Developing yourself."

It's not easy to live in the world of changing qualities, but when we do, it's truly life-altering. Several years ago, I had lunch with an amazing 20-year-old woman we'll call Paige. She had just finished a successful summer internship, and now it was fall and she was going back to school to finish her business degree. Her future was bright. She was super smart, extremely likeable, with a great attitude, and definitely going places.

Over lunch, she told me about her BIG PLAN.

It looked something like this:

Graduate business school, get job at top-tier consulting firm, get a promotion, buy condo, another promotion, get married, switch to client-side job, buy starter house, another promotion, first baby, another promotion, bigger house, second baby, promotion to C-Suite, even bigger house, buy a ski chalet at Whistler and eventually retire there.

She included the age she'd be at each stage, as well as the companies she'd work for, and the salaries and job titles she'd attain.

Listening to her, I became incredibly sad.

She'd mapped out a journey. And journeys suck. Journeys are for tourists, sitting on busses being taken from one place to another. A tourist isn't creating her experience; she's watching it happen to her.

Unstuck leaders aren't tourists. They're explorers. They're Indiana Jones. They're Lara Croft.

Unstuck leaders leave room for surprise, serendipity, uncertainty, fear and discovery. Because the truth is, our imaginations are far too limited to dream of everything that's possible for us.

Paige and I lost touch after that lunch, but I thought about her frequently over the years. I imagined her on her journey, gritting her teeth and digging in, stacking achievement upon achievement. And I worried about her. Was she happy? Was she fulfilled? Or was she stuck?

So, when I began The Unstuck Project, I found her on LinkedIn and reached out for an interview, to which she happily agreed.

It turns out, I didn't need to worry about Paige at all. And that's because the BIG PLAN is gone.

In her final year of university, Paige found herself struggling with depression. And she became stuck. She hadn't even graduated yet, and the BIG PLAN was already in jeopardy. This filled her with fear and deepened her depression. But then, Paige had a revelation. She would stop gritting her teeth and use her depression as a catalyst to rethink the whole journey thing.

The BIG PLAN was disposed of. In its place, is a new commitment to openness and experimentation. So much so, Paige is in a new city, in a new country, with a new group of friends, and a new boyfriend. Her job is in line with her goals, but her approach to getting it was completely new. It came through serendipity. A friendly meeting that led to another friendly meeting that turned into a job interview that resulted in a job offer.

"I open myself up to opportunities as they come," Paige told me. "It's been fluid and organic. Letting go of my controlled vision is what's led to new possibilities in my life."

Paige still has a general idea of what she'd like to do and accomplish in life. She's still herself, or as she put it, "I'm not going to become a yoga instructor in Bali." But at the same time, she doesn't have any specific next steps. And that's a big thing.

As she tells it, "I'm willing to go to any city in the world. I have three or four different industries that I'd be super excited about. I want the next job to be better than the last job."

If something doesn't work out, she'll move onto the next thing with no judgment or self-recrimination. There's always another path.

Paige has become watery. Hallelujah.

A Stuck Leader Reacts.
An Unstuck Leader Anticipates.

A stuck leader's entrenched, contractive state leads to intense navel gazing. That is, they lack a view of the world beyond their immediate purview.

This leads them to focus on safe problems, the kind that are nagging, but never seem to get solved. Safe problems allow stuck leaders to procrastinate, hesitate and avoid decisions. These problems create the illusion that they're working hard, without them having to face any actual risk.

This behavior leaves them blind to what's emerging around them. When a quality problem arises, the kind that involves risky, forward thinking decisions that will take the organization to a new level, they are thoroughly unprepared.

So, they react. And most often, poorly. Or as author and spiritual teacher Gary Zukav puts it, "You go nowhere by continuing to respond to the difficulties in life in the same ways that you have responded to them in the past. Your experiences change when your responses to your challenges change."

An Unstuck Leader works *on* problems, not *in* them. This means quality problems only. They don't fall into the trap of letting the urgency of endless little fires distract them from what's really important.

They're connected to their team, their customers, their suppliers and their community. They observe the goings on, both in and outside of the organization, to better understand how information flows and how decisions really get made. Their understanding of this interconnectivity and interdependency allows them to predict how a change in one system will affect the system at large.

This allows them to anticipate. And to make better decisions. And often, prevent a crisis before it even starts.

A Stuck Leader Imposes Structure.
An Unstuck Leader is a Designer.

Stuck leaders operating from an ego-system love their top-down authority. They love rules, regulations, cascading goals, performance reviews and engaging in the illusion of certainty these things give them. These leaders believe their role is to reduce tension and conflict. And one of the ways to do that is through limiting access to data and information. If no one knows what's going on, no one can form an opinion strong enough to create tension or conflict.

Another way stuck leaders seek to reduce tension and conflict is to always rely on the same metrics from the same sources of data and information. In a complex adaptive world, this creates a multitude of blind spots and emerging trends are missed.

Creating organizational silos, discouraging cross-departmental conversations and having a rigid hierarchical structure are also ways stuck leaders seek to reduce tension and conflict. If no one is talking to anyone, there's no arguing and no debating.

An Unstuck Leader sees their role as having two primary functions. First, they must enable the complex adaptive systems from which emergence, well, emerges. And second, they must act as a buffer between the administrative part of the business – legal, accounting, human resources, etc. – and the parts of the business where innovation happens.

Unstuck leaders not only prevent the administrative functions of the organization from suffocating emergence, they insist that the administrative functions adapt to the needs of those engaging in complex adaptive systems in the organization.

In balancing these the two functions of enabling leadership and administrative requirements, the Unstuck Leader must carefully design the conditions for emergence to arise, and to reap its benefits in the long-term.

The first thing the Unstuck Leader must do is embrace uncertainty. And, make it clear throughout the organization that uncertainty is not bad, it is desirable. This makes administrators, board members and other stakeholders uncomfortable. That's the point. No one should be comfortable.

Speaking of discomfort, most people find tension and conflict uncomfortable. That's a shame, because surfacing tension and conflict are a sure way to invite emergence to the table. Unstuck Leaders must ask uncomfortable questions and issue uncomfortable challenges. They must encourage uncomfortable discussions and welcome uncomfortable answers. Over time, people in the organization will become rather comfortable with the discomfort of tension and conflict. And when that fear is gone, real emergence, the game-changing kind, will begin to occur.

Unstuck Leaders encourage conversations and information sharing. They value transparency, and intelligence is distributed across the organization. In particular, Unstuck Leaders encourage conversation with and between middle managers. These are the managers who are experienced enough to really know what's going on, but not so high up in the organization that they're out of touch. They're the line managers, the people who have direct customer contact, and the people who are solving 99 percent of the organization's day-to-day issues. When middle-management is heard, the organization will focus on the real issues at hand. And, as we say in my tradition of coaching, where focus goes, energy flows.

With fear out of the picture and everyone on the same page data and information-wise, the Unstuck Leader can now encourage co-creation and iteration. No one freaks out if a project fails, they simply iterate. Over and over. Build, test, measure, adapt. When emergence occurs, the Unstuck Leader commits and mobilizes, even if what's emerging is challenging or unfamiliar.

Unstuck Leaders are excellent and inspiring storytellers who promote new ideas and solutions throughout the organization as well as externally. Emergence becomes a source of organizational pride. And it becomes the primary source of energy on which the organization thrives.

Unstuck Leaders design for diversity. Diversity of people, backgrounds, schooling and ideas. Diversity creates tension and tension creates conversations, adaptation, learning, creativity and innovation. Diversity is the surest way to avoid the perils of path dependence, making "the way we've always done it" wholly and mercifully irrelevant.

A Stuck Leader's Employees Experience Disillusionment.
An Unstuck Leader's Employees Experience Networked Independence.

The deeper a stuck leader's entrenchment into the ego-system, the more problematic their leadership becomes. Communication is unilateral. There's little tolerance for dissent. Transparency decreases. Employees are only told what they "need to know". And the focus is on the benefit of the few at the expense of employees, suppliers, customers and the community at large. This leads to organization-wide cynicism, which is the ultimate poison.

Cynical leaders and employees engage in manipulation, deluded thinking, faulty, half-hearted execution, internal competition and sabotage, and lazy decisions with little or no thought or analysis.

Employees disengage and bide their time. There's little to look forward to. There is a genuine fear of becoming "like them"; "them" being senior management.

*"Over time, I looked around and
struggled to find someone I'd be proud
to become later in life."*

– Liam, Unstuck Project interviewee

Stuck leaders have a dysfunctional relationship with failure that furthers the divide between managers and employees. When failure is unacceptable, when it is seen as the product of faulty thinking and personal weakness, employees refuse to take risks.

And that's demoralizing.

An Unstuck Leader recognizes the need to connect values and purpose to work. They develop organizational structures that allow for the *networked independence* of their teams. Employees are provided with the tools and autonomy to allow them to focus on personal development as well as long-term, sustainable growth for the organization.

When engaged in ongoing communication and feedback with their teams, Untuck Leaders listen generatively, meaning they strategically ask questions that will allow new theories, new possibilities and new actions to emerge from conversations.

Unstuck Leaders don't set the best direction. They listen for it.

A Stuck Leader Does What They Have to Do. An Unstuck Leader Does What They Want to Do.

A stuck leader doesn't think about thriving. They're focused on merely surviving. They become victims of their own fear. And that creates a tremendous gap between what they're doing each and every day and what they want to be doing every day. We're back to prioritizing *should* over *could*. And that's what makes them entrenched and stuck.

And that's a travesty for us all.

Why? Because stuck leaders are extremely adept at creating results that no one wants.[13]

Just think: what if the leaders at Facebook had fully understood and accepted their role as a media platform in the political eco-system? Would fake news be so influential and destructive?

And what if rather than entrenching themselves in old ideas, the leaders of the newspaper industry had sought to fully understand the new digital eco-system that was emerging all around them? Might they have disrupted their own business model rather than having it done to them?

What if politicians who decrease local school budgets sought to understand the supply and demand issues for future labor markets? Would every child, no matter their household income, get a chance at an impactful career?

---

[13] Scharmer and Kaufer provide an extensive analysis of "results that no one wants" in their book, *Leading From the Emerging Future*, Berrett-Koehler, 2013. Read their book, it's amazing.

All of these leaders are doing what they think they have to do. And all of them are creating results no one wants.

An Unstuck Leader spends most of their time doing what they want to do. They connect their needs, values and life purpose to their work. There is no gap between what their organization makes them do and what they want to do. This gives them much more energy and focus. And this allows them to create excellent results.

Sounds good, right?

Okay. Enough chit-chat.

HOW TO BECOME AN UNSTUCK LEADER

Over the next five chapters, I'm going to show you the five steps to becoming an Unstuck Leader.

But first, a warning.

All this Unstuck Leader stuff sounds awesome, but it's also really, really hard. And uncomfortable. And at times, exhausting. And that's why the most important type of management for the Unstuck Leader is self-management. That is to say, it's impossible to become the kind of person who does the things an Unstuck Leader does unless you're willing to do a substantial amount of inner work.

If you're not, put this book down and go watch some Netflix. If you are, here's an overview of what you're in for.

Step 1: Stop. Assess. Align.

To be an Unstuck Leader, you must understand and reclaim your authentic power; the kind of power that comes from being in alignment with your true self. Understanding your true self begins with discovering what's driving your current patterns of belief and behavior.

You've already learned about the perils of the unhealthy contractive state. In Chapter 3, we'll learn about the much more fun healthy expansive state as well as the six human needs and how they affect how we spend our time, what we focus on and ultimately, the quality of our lives. You'll explore which needs are most important to you, and the positive and negative ways you choose to fulfill them.

Next, we'll examine the qualities in life that you value (i.e. creativity, independence, knowledge, exploration, honesty, effectiveness, community). We'll arrive at three to five values that are core to who you are, and then determine what is keeping you from living them consistently. We'll use all this new self-knowledge to arrive at your purpose.

You will become watery.

Step 2: Listen and Observe.

This is where you begin your shift from an ego-system into the greater awareness of an eco-system.

Understand Others

Once you're familiar with the universal six human needs that drive our thoughts and behaviors, you'll learn how to spot them in others. With practice, care and consciousness, you'll discover how to change your communication style to meet the needs and perspectives of others. Soon, you'll find everyone around you to be absolutely fascinating. You'll discover their loves, passions, aversions and fears. You will come to genuinely care about them.

You will have credibility, trust and influence.

Understand the Whole

We tend to look at the world as a series of unrelated events. But in fact, we live in a world of interconnected systems. You've already learned about the power of Complex adaptive systems and how the enablement of them helps organizations innovate faster and more creatively. Next, you'll learn about eight *maladaptive archetypal system traps* that leaders and organizations tend to fall into. I'll show you how to recognize them and your role in creating them, as well as how to avoid them.

You will have the gift of anticipation.

Step 3: Let Go.

Letting go, or more specifically, letting go of old ideas and old ways of doing things, is terrifying to most people. Fear makes us reach into the past. The Unstuck Leader's job is not only to let go, but to make it possible for others to do so too. This creates space for what is to come.

You'll learn to let go of stability, inauthentic power structures, message control, ego, and the things in your life and business that are coming to a natural end.

You will become free to co-create the future.

Step 4: Co-create.

Once you've let go of what's ending, you'll embrace what's emerging. You'll learn the art of generative listening – working with those around you to create understanding, foster positivity and arrive at a compelling vision.

You'll learn to love tension and conflict as catalysts for creative problem solving. You'll discover new methodologies for approaching tough challenges.

This will give you the gift of innovation.

Step 5: Say Yes.

It sounds simple, but it is anything but. When you say yes to the emerging future, you also have to say yes to imperfection, boundaries, and networked connection.

You'll learn to put everything into consistent practice.

And, you'll to commit to action.

Sound good? Okay, let's get started.

Chapter 3
STEP ONE
Stop. Assess. Align.

L et's talk about power. Your power. How well would
you say you're managing it?

Each of us is powerful; though most of us don't believe
we are and act accordingly. We allow fear to make us
small, robbing us of our power. Or, that same fear leads us
to chase inauthentic, external power from pursuit of rank,
position, material possessions, and validation, or through
bullying, coercion, and manipulation.

Authentic power is not outside of you, it's internal. It's
about you, your values, your purpose and how you choose
to fulfill them. You cannot become truly powerful until
you understand your power, how you stifle it and how to
use it authentically. An authentically powerful person is a
natural, almost effortless leader.

To truly tap into our authentic power takes internal work. We must stop, assess our limiting patterns of belief and behavior, rediscover our core values and purpose, and then align our goals and actions with them.

This work is difficult and uncomfortable. You may discover some things about yourself and your past behavior that you don't like. You'll also discover how amazing, unique and talented you are. And, how truly powerful you are.

In short, you must reclaim your true self. Because you're enough. Better than enough, in fact. You're uniquely qualified to fulfill your purpose in life, whatever that may be.

THE ADULT LIFECYCLE RENEWAL PROCESS

Before we can talk about aligning with our true selves, we have to talk about the adult lifecycle renewal process. In Western society, we know an awful lot about the early years of life – we know a lot about the growth stages of infants, toddlers, preschoolers, young kids, pre-teens and teens. We also know a lot about the "firsts" of early adulthood – first jobs, first serious relationships, first years of marriage all the way through to the birth of the first child. What to expect during these phases of life is (mostly) common knowledge.

What we don't talk about, are the years between thirty-five and sixty-five. It's as if we're expected to go into some kind of thirty-year stasis in which nothing much happens. Sure, we talk about the mid-life crisis, but that's generally looked upon as an embarrassing thing that will cause a formerly rational person to suddenly lose themselves and run out to buy a sports car, a $20 thousand handbag (yes, they exist), or endure a litany of cosmetic surgery procedures.

The thing is, those years from about thirty-five to sixty-five are among the most interesting, challenging, creative and generative years of our lives. If, that is, we manage them effectively. And that requires going through a continuous series of renewal cycles.

Psychologist Frederic Hudson describes the renewal cycle as having four distinct phases: Go for it, the Doldrums, Cocooning and Getting ready.[14]

In the *Go for it* phase, we're at our best. We're prioritizing our *could* values over our *should* values. Our actions are aligned with our purpose, mission and vision. We're taking positive action toward our goals. We have a plan. We're committed and consistent. We have energy, vitality and are excited to get up and get going every day. We are in an expansive state.

The *Go for it* phase is fantastic. And because of that, most of us want to stay there indefinitely. After all, our culture has convinced us that our state of being in this phase is the only way to be if we're going to be successful. But that's impossible. If we don't burn out, we will most certainly hit a plateau. As we discussed in Chapter 1, some people are able to swim happily around in their plateaus. But for most of us, the plateau is a difficult place. It activates our fear. And in that fear, we prioritize our *should* values over our *could* values. Our needs for certainty and

---

[14] Frederic Hudson, *The Adult Years, Mastering the Art of Self-Renewal*, 1999.

significance become louder and more pressing. We slip into an unhealthy contractive state. We're stuck.

Hudson calls this stuckness, *the Doldrums*. *The Doldrums* is an unhappy, extremely uncomfortable place to be. The majority of the stuck people I spoke to in The Unstuck Project had hit a plateau and had sunk into *the Doldrums*. Their doldrums varied. They were bored, stalled or disconnected from their careers, disliked their bosses, hated the city they lived in, and a few knew they were in the wrong relationship. What they had in common was that each sensed that something was ending, and they couldn't or wouldn't move on.

The choice we make in *the Doldrums* is between holding on and letting go. Holding on is a form of self-betrayal. When we refuse to let go, we double down by avoiding change and challenge, increasing our stuckness and suffering even more. Stuckness is tedious and exhausting. And some of us seek relief in the distraction of unhealthy behaviors. We eat too much, or drink too much, slack off at work or have extramarital affairs. We might become bitter, complain a lot, or create drama around the office. We might even become gossipy or attempt to boost our self-esteem by tearing others down. And yes, this is when the so-called midlife crisis behaviors such as buying a sports car, a pricy handbag or having cosmetic surgery happen. The result is crisis – the end of a marriage, health issues, job loss and even financial ruin. All of it, because we refuse to let go.

Letting go can be sad, and is most definitely frightening, but it's also necessary. We must let go of what is ending to clear the way for something new. We need to let go of what we thought we wanted. Sometimes a dream just isn't for us. We need to let go of toxic people. Sometimes, love isn't enough. We need to let go of unfulfilling work. Nothing will deplete us faster than pointless work we aren't connected to. And, we have to let go of limiting beliefs about who and what we should be, and limiting behaviors such as procrastination, avoidance and finger-pointing.

Only when we let go, can we begin to transition. We can move to a new job, new industry, new city or country. We can start a new hobby, focus on health and wellness or go back to school. Frederic Hudson called these "micro-transitions" and we may go through several of them throughout our lives. They may seem like big changes, but in the grand scheme of things, they are superficial, small adjustments that allow us to leap back quickly into *Go for it* mode.

The really big transitions in life happen when we let go of what is most precious to us – that is, when we let go of who we think we are. And to do that, we first must enter phase three: *Cocooning*.

Rather than "Stop. Assess. Align.", this chapter could have easily been titled, "How to Cocoon". This is where shit gets real. This is the inner work I keep talking about. And it's how to transform into a true Unstuck Leader.

The process is difficult, especially if we enter into it as the result of a crisis. We may be battling depression or anxiety as we cocoon. It can be a lonely time, as those around us may not understand, or cannot understand what we're experiencing as we go through the process. We are in a contracted state, but not necessarily an unhealthy one.

Cocooning is spiritual in nature, in that it requires us to tap into our deepest, truest self. Everything is on the table during the process. Hudson says that, "Ever so gradually, you let go of the external chapter as it clings to your mind – lost dreams, lost roles, lost beauty, lost muscles, lost parents, lost careers, lost children, lost marriages, lost income, lost hope – and you live for a while in a neutral zone where you are, psychologically speaking, by yourself, in suspension, in limbo, and more aware of who you are not than who you are becoming."[15]

Okay, so yes, that does sound rather grim, but it doesn't have to be so. The purpose of this chapter is to guide you through the *Cocooning* process so that you may come to a deep understanding of yourself, what you need and what you value.

Hudson says that after the *Cocooning* process, "…you feel not merely healed but vital and alive. It is a quiet fire, within, and it brings warmth and new confidence. Your eyes mirror the resilience that you have found. You want little but feel much, and most of all you feel in touch with the deep murmurs of your own heart. Your deep-seated values arise to shape your new human agenda, and you get ready to journey again."

This is the very essence of the Unstuck Leader. And this is my wish for you. Because after you've gone through the *Cocooning* process and are aligned with your core values and purpose, you'll enter Phase Four of Hudson's lifecycle renewal process: *Getting ready.*

What are we getting ready for? Our emergence as a new kind of leader. An Unstuck Leader. And with that, a new

---

[15] Hudson, *The Adult Years*, 65.

life chapter of exploration. In *Getting ready*, we take our new selves for a test drive. We meet new people, learn new things, ask new questions. We plot a new course. One that is aligned with who we are.

And eventually, we will hit another plateau. And maybe we'll swim around in it for a while, and maybe we'll sink into t*he Doldrums*. And maybe a micro-transition will do the trick to transport us back into *Go for it* mode, and maybe we'll need to *Cocoon* again. And then *Get Ready* again. And then *Go for it* again.

And on and on the cycle goes, and with each revolution, we emerge with new capabilities, new wisdom, more confidence and a deeper reservoir of purpose and meaning. And through it all, we accept that this is the cycle of life in the adult years and through that acceptance, we remain unstuck.

HEALTHY EXPANSIVE STATE. HEALTHY CONTRACTIVE STATE.

The renewal process is a cycling, not only through the four phases, but also through both the healthy expansive and healthy contractive states. We're meant to expand and contract, just as we're meant to breathe, and our hearts are meant to pump. The warmth and growth of summer is followed by the cold and hibernation of winter. Expansion and contraction are a part of the natural order of things. And they're a part of us.

When we're in *Go for it* mode, we're in a healthy expansive state. Healthy expansion is about growing and contributing. When we're expansive, we focus on positive things. We're curious and eager. We want to help others. We use positive language both when speaking to ourselves and to others. We're relaxed and open, but with a strong core.

Think of a dancer. She can't do a great pirouette if her shoulders are hunched up and her core muscles are disengaged. She'll lose her balance and fall over. Her chest needs to be relaxed and open and her core needs to be strong. Same for athletes. Relaxed, chest open, shoulders down, with a strong core ensures peak performance and minimizes injury. Same goes for all of us on a metaphorical level. If we have a closed heart and we ignore our core values, we'll contract. If we have an open heart and strong core values, we'll expand.

There's also such a thing as an unhealthy expansive state. If a balloon keeps expanding and expanding and expanding, eventually, it will pop. So will we. We don't want that for ourselves, that's not what we're going for here. Yet, the world is full of popped balloons.

Chef Albert Adria was the creative director at elBulli, the most famous restaurant in the world. Though not as well-known as his brother, head chef Ferran Adria, Albert was equally responsible for elBulli's success. Each season, Albert was charged with creating forty-five innovative, rule-breaking, thoroughly original, not to mention delicious dishes. Forty-five! And he did it. Year after year, season after season until eventually, he popped. He just couldn't do it anymore.

Albert's mind, his creativity and his passion for his work were completely depleted. And wisely, to save himself, he did the unthinkable. He quit the best restaurant in the world. And in doing so, he allowed himself to contract. After a time of cocooning and rejuvenation, Albert re-entered an expansive state, this time on his own terms. Albert is now the creative force behind six restaurants. He calls his restaurant group elBarri "A gastronomic amusement park". Pretty expansive sounding.

Unstuck Project interviewee Myles, a CEO, had a very successful business, until the financial crisis of 2008. Then, everything changed, except for Myles. He refused to change the way he did business. "My ego blinded me to the signs that seemed obvious to retrench. And instead, I doubled down and invested in some businesses and some real estate. The result was pretty swift. I was in another city, about to win an award for being a top performer in my industry. I was in my hotel room alone, just prior to the event, all gussied up. And I had a major meltdown. I couldn't stop crying. Two hours later, I was standing in front of a ballroom full of people. I stood there, and knew I was crashing."

Looking back, Myles admits that he was unwilling to allow people to see that he was failing. He was unwilling to accept the embarrassment and pain of it. So, he kept going, and going, and going, until he popped. "In hindsight," he told me, "I wish my speech was about vulnerability and acceptance of where I was in my life."

In Myles's mind, it wasn't okay to contract. But he couldn't stop it. Eventually, he fell into a deeply unhealthy contractive state that left him stuck and depressed and drinking too much. He nearly lost his wife as a result.

So, is there such a thing as a healthy contraction? You bet. When you're sick and you go to bed for a few days of ginger ale and chicken soup, that's a healthy and necessary contraction. A beer with co-workers after a successful pitch meeting is a healthy contraction. A walk around the block after drama with your teenager is a healthy contraction, as is a week on a beach with a margarita and a John Grisham novel. And, slipping into the *Cocooning* phase of the life renewal cycle is a healthy contraction.

Myles did just that. To begin his healing process, he went on a seven-day leadership retreat. He couldn't really afford it, but he knew he had to do it. It was the beginning of something. Eventually Myles learned meditation and over the next year or two, he embarked on a slow journey of getting to know himself. And eventually, he started a new business, and did well with it.

Throughout the rest of this chapter, I'll show you how to expand and contract in a healthy way as you move through the life renewal cycle. And it begins with understanding your six human needs.

THE SIX HUMAN NEEDS

Before we can begin to understand the limiting patterns of belief and behavior that may be keeping us stuck, we have to understand how we are fulfilling, or not fulfilling our six human needs. These needs drive our behavior, whether we're aware of it or not. And each of us prioritizes their fulfillment in different ways, which can be positive or negative and can lead to internal and external conflict.

Let's start with Maslow's Hierarchy of needs.[16] If you've ever taken a psychology, sociology or marketing class, you've heard of it.

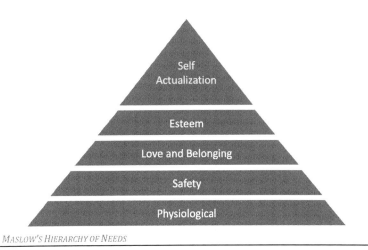

MASLOW'S HIERARCHY OF NEEDS

Our lowest level needs are *Physiological*. To survive, we all need food, water, shelter, oxygen, rest, and activity. Next, are our *Safety* needs. We need to be protected from potentially dangerous things, people or situations, both physically and psychologically. After that are our needs for *Love and Belonging*. We need to give and receive love, affection, trust and acceptance. And we need to feel that we're a part of a community. Our next set of needs are for *Esteem*. We need to know that we matter, we're respected and that we're competent. At the top, is the need for *Self-*

[16] Maslow, A. (1943). A Theory of Human Motivation. *Psychological Review*, 50(4), pp.370-396.

Actualization. This is the need to reach our ultimate potential.

Even if you learned the hierarchy of needs in school, you may not know that later in life, Maslow went back and added three more needs.[17]

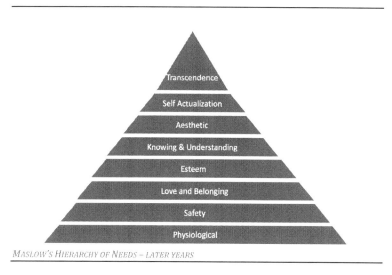

MASLOW'S HIERARCHY OF NEEDS – LATER YEARS

He added the need for *Knowing and Understanding.* We need to have our curiosity satisfied. We need to explore. We need meaning.[18] He added the *Aesthetic* needs. This is the need to have beauty in our lives. Art, nature, symmetry, balance, order and form all meet our aesthetic needs. I love that Maslow believed that we need these things in our lives rather than simply wanting them. And he added the need for *Transcendence* to the top of the

---

[17] Maslow, A., *Motivation and Personality*, 1954, Second ed. 1970. Third ed. 1987.

[18] I suspect this is why many of you picked up this book in the first place.

hierarchy. This is the need to help others self-actualize and reach their full potential.

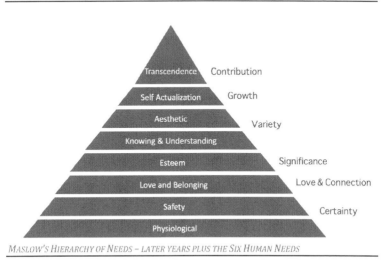

MASLOW'S HIERARCHY OF NEEDS – LATER YEARS PLUS THE SIX HUMAN NEEDS

The six human needs we talk about in Strategic Intervention coaching are complementary to Maslow's hierarchy.

We see the physiological needs as the need for *Certainty*. We see the need for love and belonging exactly as Maslow did, only we tend to call it *Love and Connection*. The esteem needs are referred to as the need for *Significance*. The cognitive and aesthetic needs are called the need for *Variety* (or uncertainty). The need for self-actualization is referred to as the need for *Growth* and the need for transcendence is referred to as the need for *Contribution*.

The first four: certainty, love and connection, significance and variety are the base-level needs. Everyone experiences them. The top two needs: growth and contribution, are the higher-level, or spiritual needs.

Generally, you have to be doing pretty well at meeting the base-level needs before you put your focus on the higher-level needs.

Let's have a look at each of the needs in greater detail.

Certainty

As we discussed in Chapter 1, certainty is the trickiest of all the needs, because it arises from the most primitive parts of our brains – the reptilian brain, which is mostly interested in keeping the lights on, and the paleomammalian brain, where our emotions reside. The trouble with certainty is that we are biologically built for survival, not truth. And our judgements are often faulty as a result.

Certainty is all about comfort, security, stability, predictability, and feeling grounded, safe and protected.

There's nothing inherently bad about our need for certainty. It can most definitely keep us from making dumb-ass decisions. But it can also cause us to engage in behaviors that reduce our authentic power. And those behaviors are the result of fear. Staying in a dead-end job, going along to get along, remaining in an unsatisfying relationship, shying away from risk, failing to stand up for what we believe is right and other inauthentic behaviors are the result of a high need for certainty.

Leaders who demand certainty are likely to lead risk-averse organizations where debate, dissent, ingenuity and inventiveness are stifled. When things don't go to plan, the certainty-needing leader may resort to blame and finger-pointing, even if circumstances are beyond the control of the people being pointed at. In addition to feeling near constant fear, these leaders are also frequently frustrated by, and in constant battle with, the world's inherent uncertainty. They are, in effect, condemned to a lifetime of fighting imaginary enemies.

Unstuck Leaders feel the need for certainty as much as anybody else; sometimes profoundly so. But unlike a stuck leader, they learn to thrive despite it. They become curious about their need for certainty. What's causing it? Why now? What can be done to alleviate it? Working through these questions requires them to become vulnerable and discuss their fear with the people in their lives, both in the organization and outside of it. This doesn't mean bleeding all over their team members. It means admitting when they don't have all the answers and standing comfortably in that truth. And it means, returning to their core values and purpose so that even when things get a little shaky, they have a path forward.

Significance

As with certainty, we talked a lot about the need for significance in earlier chapters. It is, like most of the other needs, a double-edged sword. A high need for significance can lead to the achievement of amazing, seemingly impossible things. And that's great, if those things benefit others. Barack Obama, Bill Gates and Jane Goodall have a high need for significance. But so does Harvey Weinstein. Nuff said.

Significance is about pride, importance, standards (if someone has really high standards, that's a significance thing), achievement and performance. Perfectionism is also a significance thing. And so is competitiveness.

We fulfill our need for significance in positive ways by creating or building things, helping others or doing meaningful work. Or, we can fulfill this need by tearing someone else down. We can become showboaty or boastful. We can demand respect and attention.

Our culture places great emphasis on the significance of leaders. We co-create unhealthy narcissism in the people in charge by worshiping them as visionaries and operators while simultaneously not calling them out for poor behavior. Unchecked, the leader is unable to see beyond their needs. Nothing matters but their own gratification leading to shallow values and minimal intellectual interest. This is the anathema to functioning in a complex adaptive system where intent listening and understanding are imperatives.

An Unstuck Leader learns to transcend their need for significance and/or channel it toward positive things. They are more interested in an idea or strategy than who came up with it. They are more interested in results than accolades for performance. They cultivate personal humility, not because they feel less than others, but because they take joy in knowing that each of us has a unique talent and ability and if discovered and nurtured that talent and ability will benefit us all.

Love and Connection

Everyone strives for love and connection. This need continues throughout our lives. Even if we don't experience romantic love, we can have ways of feeling connected to others through our community, workplace and through service.

Love and connection is about togetherness, unity, warmth, tenderness, desire, passion and cherishing (which is a lovely word, don't you think?).

Positive ways of meeting this need are being a devoted friend, cultivating family relationships, or if that's not the right thing for you, building a new family from your circle of friends. You can meet this need through volunteering, being a part of a well-functioning team and of course, through a healthy romantic relationship. Negative ways of meeting your need for love and connection are being manipulative, demanding, duplicitous or overly needy.

As anyone who's ever watched *The Office* knows, leaders who are overly needy and require their employees and colleagues to love them, are going to get stuck. Great team comradery is one thing, but when a leader *needs* to be loved, it affects their ability to make good decisions as they can be easily manipulated by shrewd players. Also, when a needy leader feels they're not getting the love they deserve, it can reduce their productivity and make them vindictive toward those who they consider to be the guilty, love-withholding parties.

An Unstuck Leader focusses on connection, not love. They make an effort to understand the people they work with. They're deeply empathetic and are able to consider the complexities of the organization from multiple perspectives. This creates loyal employees who stick around for the long-haul. These long-tenure employees develop deep knowledge, experience and professional instincts, making them better prepared to spot what's emerging and adapt to changes and challenges in the systems they're a part of.

Variety

We need new things in our lives. We need variety to feel joy, to feel vital and to be innovative. If someone is caught in a dull day-to-day routine, they will just naturally begin seeking change and looking for uncertainty, even if it's completely unrelated to their work. We do this because we need variety to feel alive.

Variety is about fear (watching a scary movie can make you feel more alive), suspense, change, entertainment, newness, excitement, conflict and crisis.

Positive ways of meeting our need for variety include reading and learning new things, traveling, creating art, meeting new people, and challenging oneself with a new project. Sometimes, a Netflix binge will even do the trick.

Negative ways of getting variety include risky behaviors such as extremely dangerous sports (think base jumping or ice wall climbing). We can get variety from food and that's fine, unless we become overdependent on food for this purpose and end up overeating on a regular basis. Drugs and alcohol can be excellent sources of variety because they make the world seem different. Risky sexual behaviors and other forms of compulsivity such as shoplifting, or overspending provide variety. Creating drama is a fantastic source of variety. If you have a drama queen or king in your life, chances are, they're bored off their ass.

Leaders with a high need for variety that isn't properly managed can be exhausting to work with as they leap around from project to project and interest to interest. They change their minds rapidly and constantly, leaving employees trying to keep up.

Unstuck Leaders love variety too. They find it everywhere. They're interested in people and places and ideas. They never stop learning and are able to combine disparate fields of knowledge and information into ground breaking strategies and products. In other words, Unstuck Leaders channel their need for variety into growth.

Growth

Growth is a higher form of variety seeking. Variety is about happiness. It's fleeting. Growth is about fulfillment. It's lasting. What makes growth fulfilling is that it's grounded in intention.

We need to constantly develop – intellectually, emotionally and spiritually. All the good things in life, be they healthy relationships, happiness or love must be cultivated, developed and expanded or they go away.

Growth is about learning, expanding, evolving, developing, improving, advancing and stretching.

The positive ways of meeting this need are endless. Taking courses, reading, travelling, volunteering, making connections with new kinds of people, and encountering new situations and challenges. Unless our need for growth causes us to ignore our base level needs, or if we become overly obsessive on a topic in a way that damages other parts of our lives, there really aren't any negative ways to meet this need.

Contribution

I love contribution. It's the grandmother of all the other needs.

Contribution is the need to go beyond ourselves and our base needs to give to others. Life is incomplete without it, it's essential to fulfillment and happiness, but many people never focus here. They stay wrapped up in their lower needs for certainty and significance and never move beyond. But here's the thing: when we focus on something beyond ourselves, most of our problems and sources of pain become less significant. There's a magic that happens when you get outside of yourself and focus on what's going on with other people.

Contribution is about giving, volunteering, caring, empathy, compassion, grace and philanthropy.

The best thing about contribution is that it regulates the other needs.

If we're focused on contribution, we have the certainty of knowing we're on the right path. This is the only real form of certainty, because all other forms are an illusion – they can vanish at any moment. But the certainty of knowing we're living the life we were meant to live is pretty special. We get variety, because by nature, contribution is highly interactive. We're helping other people. And depending on the kind of contribution we choose, we can get variety from creative problem solving as well. We feel significant because we know we're having a positive impact on the world. We experience love and connection from the spiritual bond that comes from helping others. And we grow from figuring out new, ingenious ways of doing so. We also gain a greater understanding of ourselves in the process.

Let's have a look at your needs. The exercise below is designed to help you identify them and address them in healthy ways.

EXERCISE: WHAT DO YOU NEED?

Contemplate the six human needs in your life.

On a scale of 1 to 10, score how well each of your needs is being met.

Certainty – to feel safe and avoid pain

Love and Connection – to give and receive love, and to be a part of a community

Significance – the need to feel that we matter

Variety – the need for newness to feel alive

Growth – to learn and expand

Contribution – to help others fulfill their needs

Which needs are best met (score of 7 or higher)?

What are you doing to meet those needs?

Are all of your ways positive?

Are there any negative ways you're meeting those needs?

Note: It's okay if none of your needs are being met at a score of 7 or higher. That's in part what we're going to address in this chapter.

Which needs have the lowest scores?

What are you doing to meet those needs?

Are all of your ways positive?

Are there any negative ways you're meeting those needs?

What would have to happen for you to feel that your needs are being met at a level 8 or 10?

Are your expectations realistic?

For example: If, to feel significant, you need all of your work colleagues to acknowledge your accomplishments in writing... is that realistic? Is there another way you could feel significant without external validation?

Or: if to feel certainty, you need to know you'll succeed before you begin any project... is that realistic? Is there a

way you could change the way you look at the project –
perhaps as an exploration, rather than a quest for a specific
outcome?

*Which two needs do you feel are the most
important to you at this time in your life?*

Why do you think they're the most important?

What small steps can you take immediately to begin to
better fulfill those needs?

ALL ABOUT VALUES

Values are simply your personal judgement of what is
important in your life. Needs are often the architects of
values and vice versa. When you find a way to meet a
need, continuing to meet it can become a value that you
make a priority in your life. Or, if you have a value that
isn't being met, you may feel a driving need to fulfill it.

For example, if you learn to meet your need for
certainty by putting away ten percent of your income each
month, financial responsibility may become a value.
Alternatively, if financial responsibility is something you
value, but you're experiencing turmoil in your financial
life, your need for certainty may come roaring to your
attention.

Or, if you meet your need for variety by writing short
stories or painting, or seeking out particularly difficult

problems to solve, and you find this fulfilling, living a creative life may become a value you prioritize in your life. Alternatively, if you're in a boring job that doesn't allow creative expression, your need for variety may pop its head up.

When a need is met, we live from the value it creates, rather than being driven by it. And this is incredibly freeing! We're living it. We're not being driven by anything. It's a part of us and it radiates through us.

And this is critical because when a need is not met, and we're driven by it, we may be tempted to fulfill it in negative ways. And when we fulfill our needs in negative ways, we're essentially running away from our values. In doing this, we're betraying ourselves. And this takes a terrible toll on us spiritually, emotionally and even physically.

When we live in harmony with our values, we feel less stress and more joy. We are more confident because of the certainty we gain from knowing we're living our lives as we were meant to. We become expansive.

When we're not living our values, we contract. There's less of us.

Okay, so you may be feeling a little uncomfortable right now. What are values? What are your values? This may be something you've never stopped and considered before.

Let's start by talking about the three types of values.[19] We learned about *should* and *could* values in Chapter 1. But there's also a third type and those are the *core* values.

Should values are the superficial things we think we should believe and do. They're imposed upon us and we

---

[19] Williams and Menendez, *Becoming a Professional Life Coach*, 217.

learn them from a young age. They can be banal things such as "be polite" and "respect your elders". Sometimes though, they can be corrosive, such as "don't speak up" or "don't rock the boat".

I'm not a big fan of the *should* values. I think they're connected to our base fears – fear of loss, fear of less and fear of never. And at the core of those fears is the belief that we're not enough and ultimately that we aren't worthy of love. *Should* values are external. They're not a part of us the way our *could* values are.

Our *could* values are the personal values we choose for ourselves and they resonate with us on a deep level. There's an endless list of these values, but in reviewing various writings on values, master coaches Patrick Williams and Diane Menendez conclude that *could* values typically fall into three categories: Experiencing, Creating and Being.[20]

The Experiencing values are related to how we act and what we experience in the world. Examples are freedom, exploration, nurturing, and accountability.

The Creating values are about what we bring into existence (I love that phrase). Examples are designing, playing, expressing, innovating and, of course, creating.

The Being values are about our attitudes, mindsets and quality of character. These values are a very big deal. They encompass things such as integrity, authenticity, peace and openness.

From our *could* values, there's usually a list of three to five that are most important to us. Those are our *core* values. Think of them as our personal North Star. It's in

---

[20] Ibid, 223.

honoring these values that we express our truest selves and live our best lives.

So, you can see why this stuff is so important.

Unstuck Project interviewee Lucas used his *core* values to implement a system that allows him to stay in alignment. He says, "It starts with what I call my overarching goals. They're the things that are important to me from a generalist point of view. What are my dreams, and what am I optimizing for? If something isn't optimizing one of my drivers, I won't do it."

Lucas's values are: be happy, be known, be financially free, be fit and strong, and be loved.

Similarly, interviewee Isaac, has what he calls his "Five Pillars": family first, impact on country, always be learning, work with great people, trust your gut.

How do we identify our values? Well, there are internal clues. They're in the things we like to do. They're in the times when we're at our best. They're in what we were like as kids. They're in what has made us successful in the past. And they're in what we'd like more of in our lives. Not surprisingly, our friends and family have a good idea of what our values are as we display them on a daily basis. Once we consider all of these things, the secret is to look for the commonalities.

I should mention too, that our values are likely to change over time. This is often related to life stage. Early in our career, we might place high value on achievement, independence and status. If we have young children, love, safety and security come to the forefront. Then, in our forties, fifties and beyond, spiritual values such as service, creativity and peace begin to arise.

EXERCISE: WHAT DO YOU VALUE?

List 10 activities that bring you joy or satisfaction in your life.

What are the common ingredients that are present in these things?

List 10 times in the past 5 years when you felt you were being or performing at your best.

What are the common ingredients that are present in these things?

List 10 things you're grateful for in your life.

Looking back at your career and your life, what habits, circumstances, personal qualities or situations have made you successful?

Would you say those things are a healthy force in your life?

Think back to when you were 10 years old (or there about).

What were your defining qualities?
What do you like about that little person?

Have those qualities remained a part of you?

Are there qualities you nurtured as you matured?

Are there qualities you stifled as you matured?

What are the things that you want more of in your life?

Take a moment to review your answers from the six human needs exercise.

Of the needs you are meeting at a high level, what values are being created?

Of the needs you're not meeting at a high level, what values are being created?

How might your answers to the above questions reveal your values?

Refer to the list of values available at this link: judysims.com/values

Circle 10 or more words to which you're drawn.

Are there any words that aren't listed that you'd like to add?

These are your *could* or *chosen* Values.

When you look at the list, does it resonate with you?

Ask people who you trust and who know you well to name your values.

Ask questions to clarify. This is no time for misunderstanding.

Do any of their answers resonate with you?

Take a few days to reflect on your values.

Review your list of values one more time.

Which 3 to 5 are the most important to you?

These are your *core* values.

You'll know you've hit on your core values when you feel a sense of relief. You now know what's important to you. You have a roadmap for living your life. Write your values down and put them where you will see them every day. You might want to make them the lock screen on your phone, or the wallpaper on your computer.

PURPOSE

Now that we know what you need and what you value, let's talk about your purpose in life.

Feeling uncomfortable? Yeah, me too. After all, we're only talking about the underlying reason for being that gives your life meaning. No biggie.

Most of us avoid lofty topics such as "life purpose". Running around telling everyone about your God-given life purpose is obnoxious isn't it? Besides, what makes you so special? Who the hell are you to have a purpose?

Not everyone feels that way of course. Aristotle (you may have heard of him), didn't see purpose as lofty or divine. He saw it as a responsibility. He posited that we're here on earth to promote "human flourishing", both our own, and that of others. To him, flourishing is the highest good, and all actions must aim toward it.

So, from Aristotle's perspective, the real question isn't: Who the hell are you to have a purpose, it's *Who the hell are you to deny your purpose?*

Hmm. Maybe we should talk about purpose after all.

Chances are, you've already had plenty of times in your life when you were *on purpose*. Think of the times you were at your absolute best. Think of the times you've lost yourself in your work or found yourself in a state of flow. That's purpose.

Your purpose isn't about anyone but you. It's the thing that gives meaning to your life, not what others think you should do with your life. And, it doesn't have to be earth shattering. Some of the most successful, impactful people in the world have purposes that on the surface, are seemingly small.

Check out these humble purposes:

To be happy and make others happy.

- The Dalai Lama

To be a teacher. And to be known for inspiring my students to be more than they thought they could be.

- Oprah Winfrey[21]

To be a friend to anyone who needs one.

-   Magali Peysha, co-creator of the Strategic Intervention coaching methodology

---

I always fall a little in love with my clients when they reveal their purpose to me, because I get to see a glimpse of their core essence.

I've thought a lot about my purpose over the years and I've come to realize that I'm at my best when I'm creating. I've gravitated to creative pursuits my entire career, culminating in my current roles as a coach and writer. Coaching is a remarkably creative occupation, which is

---

[21] Yeah, there's a hint of Oprah's high need for significance that purpose statement. But in her defence, she chooses to channel it in a way that benefits others.

one of the many reasons I was drawn to it. And it was in coaching training that I arrived at my purpose:

To live a creative life, and to help others do so too.

When we're clear on our purpose, it's in us, it's a part of us and it affects each and every decision we make, often unconsciously. When we take action in support of our purpose, we do so from a place of authenticity and vital energy. We find it easier to take risks. We're more confident setting boundaries. We're less petty and more generous with others, and their trust in us grows.

It really is magical.

Just remember, the goal is not perfection. The goal is exploration.

Because the truth is, all this needs and values and purpose stuff is about possibilities. When we're open to possibilities, we get to live a fully explored life. An expansive life. How wonderful.

EXERCISE: FINDING YOUR PURPOSE

List 5 to 10 times in your life when you believe you were on purpose.

These are the times when you felt aligned with your inner self and were performing at your best. You might have been experiencing a sense of flow, or been so absorbed in the moment, you lost track of time.

Use your gut. You may not be able to articulate exactly what it was that made you feel purposeful. That's okay.

Write your list quickly. Don't overthink this.

Examples may be from your childhood, your career, your personal life, times when you were traveling, creating, learning, teaching, etc.

You can choose examples from the entire span of your life, but if possible, give particular focus to the last five to ten years.

Thinking of those purposeful moments, write a few sentences about being on purpose.

What was the situation?

How did it feel?

Did you know you were *on purpose*, or in flow at the time, or do you only recognize it now, upon reflection?

Were you alone or with other people?

Was there a positive or negative outcome to your purposefulness? Or was it simply a moment in time? What about the purposeful experience was valuable to you?

Looking at your notes, what are the key ingredients that led you to feeling that you were on purpose?

You may find words or phrases that you used repeatedly in describing your purposeful moments. There may be situations or people who appear again and again.

Was there a word or phrase that felt particularly powerful to you, even if you only used it once?

Give it a try. Write a purpose statement. Just one or two sentences.

No perfectionism allowed!

Your statement is about you and no one else.

It can be small or lofty. That's up to you, because it's about you.

How does it feel? Does it fit?

Read your purpose statement aloud.

Does it give you clarity?

Do you feel connected to it?

Is it aligned with your Core Values?

Does the idea of fulfilling it give you energy, rather than drain you of it?

Would you print it on a t-shirt or coffee mug?

Does the idea of acting in line with it give you joy?

If you answered yes to all of the above, good for you!

If not, give yourself a break of a few days or even weeks. And then try again. You'll get there!

WHAT'S HOLDING YOU BACK?

"What does stuckness mean? A state of mind as I can understand. It comes from the inside out. It's a reaction, not a function of the outside world."

– Mitch, Unstuck Project interviewee.

I don't know about you, but I have a little voice in my head. One that seems to know better than me. It popped up a lot during my first marriage. And then when I was a corporate vice president. And again, when I was a start-up CEO.

Each time, the voice said, "This isn't me".

And it was right. I was very unhappy in all of those situations. Yet, there I was, in those situations.

We all have a little part of ourselves that sees clearer than the rest of us does. Some call it the soul. Some call it the observer. I call it the true self. And it's pretty amazing.

But many of us fear our true selves, because the true self is a dangerous thing. Being our true selves requires risk. And risk is scary and awful and we'd rather just not.

So, we stuff our true selves down deep into our subconsciousness. And we forget who we are. And we feel lost and frustrated. We shrink away from life's challenges. We shrink away from possibilities. Instead of creating our lives, we simply react to people and situations.

In other words, we give up our authentic power.

And we get stuck.

Why on earth do we do this to ourselves?

Well, it seems there's two culprits. First, we allow our needs (usually certainty and significance are the troublemakers) to drive us out of alignment with our values and purpose. And second, we chose to distract ourselves from fulfilling our values and purpose with insignificant safe problems rather than focusing on risky, life-changing quality problems.

Let's have a closer look at each.

Values Conflicts: When What You're Doing Doesn't Align with Who You Are

I once had a wonderful, kind, creative, brilliant client we'll call Janice. Janice had a big job at a very prestigious organization. One would think she would have been fulfilled. But she wasn't. Janice came to me because she didn't like who she was when she was at work. Janice worked fifty or more hours per week, and all of that time, was spent in a state of self-loathing.

I was determined to help Janice work through her problem, so we started with some values exercises. After some time and introspection, she arrived at a set of *core* values: curiosity, creativity, integrity, effectiveness and independence. These are awesome values! How could someone who has these values not like who she is when she's at work?

I asked Janice what had to happen for her to feel these values were being upheld. And this is where it got interesting.

For curiosity and creativity, she had to feel that she had the freedom to explore and experiment in her role. Due to the culture of her organization, this was not possible.

For her to feel integrity, she needed to know that the things she was doing had a net benefit to the world, and that she wasn't lying, cheating or hurting anyone. But at her organization, there was a lot of gossip and bitter, nasty talk disguised as venting. And Janice bought into it. Sometimes she engaged in those behaviors too. I want to reiterate that Janice is a wonderful person. She's kind and thoughtful. But, being in the wrong environment, one that didn't support her values, made her betray her own nature.

For Janice to feel effective, she needed some kind of accomplishment. But in her organization, projects were frequently scrapped mid-way through. She often felt her work was pointless. This was, of course, demoralizing.

And, for Janice to feel independent, she needed her decisions to be respected. And, from what I've already told you about this organization, I don't think you'll be surprised to learn that wasn't happening.

So I asked her, "How many of your values are supported in your current job?"

And after a long pause, she answered, "None of them."

And that's why Janice didn't like who she was at work.

As we worked through just how exactly Janice found herself in this position, she came to realize that her high need for certainty kept her in a place she hated and caused her to betray her *core* values. And this betrayal was holding her back from the things she wanted most in her life.

We talked about unhealthy and healthy contractive states, and soon Janice was cocooning, getting to know herself again. And eventually, she quit her job. Talk about challenging your need for certainty! She did it, because she knew she couldn't continue as she was. She was no longer willing to betray herself. Janice took six months to travel and journal and re-evaluate. She needed that time to discover what she really wanted out of life.

Do you have to quit your job to get back into alignment with your core values and purpose? No. But you do have to give yourself the time and space to do the internal work required. You can begin with the exercise on the next page.

EXERCISE: WHERE ARE YOUR VALUES CONFLICTED?

Refer to your list of core values. What has to happen for you to feel that those values are being met?

For example, if one of your values is independence, what has to happen for you to feel independent?

Given what has to happen, how likely is it that your values will be upheld?

Are the things that need to happen realistic? For example, if to feel achievement at work, you need your boss to acknowledge you each and every day… is that realistic? Do you need to change your view on what has to happen so that it's more realistic?

How well does your current life situation, career, relationship, etc. support your values?

For example, if to feel innovative, you need freedom to explore new ideas, but your current job doesn't allow that… is your job supporting your values?

Take a look at last week's calendar. Highlight the times you were living your values.

Take a look at next week's calendar. Highlight the times you will be living your values.

List 3 to 5 places where you're out of alignment.

What are the situations that are most likely to take you out of alignment?

Are those situations primarily at home, at work, or both?

Are there certain people or types of people around whom you find yourself out of alignment?

What are the signs that you might be out of alignment?

Stress?
Anxiety?
An urge to numb with food, alcohol, YouTube, porn, mindless scrolling, etc.?
A feeling of disconnection from self or others?

Look at your list of core values. List 5 ways you want to feel every day when in alignment.

For example, calm, joyful, excited, intellectually stimulated, loved, loving, fulfilled, spiritual, healthy, vital, etc.

How can you begin to move yourself back into alignment?

Are there behaviors you can change?

Can you change the dynamics of certain relationships?

Are there situations you can avoid?

Are there situations you can seek?

The Problem with Problems: When You Distract Yourself from Risk and Change

In Chapter 1, we talked about safe problems and quality problems. Quality problems involve a risky, forward thinking decision that will take us to a new level or life stage. They're scary for sure, but they're solvable. And in solving them, we experience growth. Ain't nothing wrong with a good quality problem. In fact, a true Unstuck Leader spends a good amount of time looking for quality problems to solve. This is how we create tension in an organization. And it's how ingenuity, resourcefulness and inventiveness emerge.

Safe problems on the other hand, allow us to procrastinate, hesitate and avoid decisions. They're the lingering issues in our lives that never seem to get fixed. We secretly love our safe problems. We keep them because they create the illusion that we're working hard, without us having to face any actual risk. That's why when we face a risky decision (or a quality problem), we'll often develop a safe problem to distract ourselves. We might say, "I can't become a public speaker until I lose twenty pounds". Or, "I can't decide on what to do until I have every last piece of data possibly available." Or, "I can't fire that employee until after Thanksgiving, Christmas, Valentine's Day, St. Patrick's Day…".

Safe problems are insidious. We're rarely aware that we're using them as a mental crutch. I once watched a colleague miss an important launch deadline for his website because he was agonizing over a barely noticeable difference in the font size of his logo. In that moment, he felt a deep urgency to get the font size right. He didn't think, "Hey, it's a website, I can change the font on the logo any time I want!". He created his safe problem to distract him from the scary quality problem of launching a new website, one that may or may not be successful.

When a safe problem happens to meet two or more of our base level needs, the real trouble begins, because it serves us so well. Safe problems provide the certainty that they'll never be solved, and therefore, we'll never have to face the terror of the quality problem. They provide love and connection because we can talk to friends and loved ones and sometimes perfect strangers about our problems and receive all kinds of delicious sympathy in return. They provide the variety of an excellent distraction from our very scary quality problems. And can be quite useful for making us feel significant. As in, woe is me, I have a Really Big Problem. Let me tell you all about it.

Think you don't have any safe problems? Well, I'll bet you do. Why don't you do the exercise below and we'll see who's right?

EXERCISE: SAFE PROBLEMS

Make a list of all the nagging issues or problems in your life that just don't seem to get resolved.

Do you have problems:

- At home?
- At the office?
- In your relationships?

- In your health?
- On a particular project?

How are these problems serving you?

For each problem, consider what may be the quality problem you're avoiding.

How would it feel if you overcame your safe problems?

How would your life change?
When you think of that change, do you feel fearful, energized, relieved, anxious?

Why do you think you feel that way? Hint: go back to your needs and values analyses.

Make a plan to once and for all, solve one of your safe problems

Start with the smallest or the largest, it's up to you.

Chapter 4
STEP TWO
Listen and Observe

Step 1 was very much about the ego-system. We took a look inward at our deepest drivers, motivations, values and purpose to arrive at an understanding of who we are and how we want to be in the world.

Now it's time to think about the eco-system. Your organization is a system of systems within systems. And each system is profoundly influenced by the individuals who operate within them. We each come to work with personal systems of internal needs, values and purpose and our motivations and performance are affected accordingly. Groups of individuals also form systems of collective needs, values and purpose and their motivations and performance are also affected accordingly. These systems arise vertically and horizontally and sometimes randomly across the organization.

If all this sounds complex, that's because it is. But to deny this complexity is what leads to the types of tone-deaf top-down leadership that creates disengagement and cynicism in the organization.

When we understand how the various systems arise, operate and disintegrate, we have the gift of anticipation.

UNDERSTANDING OTHERS

We All Have Our Stuff. And We Bring it to Work.

Author, CEO and meditation teacher, Michael Singer, refers to our internal disturbances as our "inner thorns".[22] He asks us to imagine a thorn in our arm that directly touches a nerve. The thorn hurts when it's touched, and over time, it becomes a serious problem. So, we build an infrastructure around it so no one can ever touch it. The thorn of course, represents the traumas, hurts and losses that occur over the course of any life. We could act to remove the thorn by coming to terms with the life events that created it, but most of us are afraid to. And soon, our whole lives revolve around protecting the thorn and avoiding pain. Freud would have called our attempts to protect the thorn, our defence mechanisms. We all have our thorns, and we bring them, and the defense mechanisms we create to protect them, to work.

---

[22] Michael Singer, *The Untethered Soul*, 2007, 128.

Remember those six human needs? Yeah, they come to work too. And so do our healthy and unhealthy ways of meeting them. We also bring our values and purpose to work. And, we bring our perfectionisms, boundaries, fear and other holdbacks as well. And together, in teams both permanent and temporary, we collectively create thorns, needs, values, purposes, perfectionisms, boundaries, fear and holdbacks.

With all this "stuff" going on, organizations become bubbling cauldrons of both conscious and unconscious human desires and fears that have little to do with corporate vision or strategy. Employees are not only distracted by the cauldron, but their creative energy and focus are dissolved within it, and they become essentially unavailable to us as leaders. Organizational theorist Gareth Morgan calls this "unconscious collusion that taps shared fears, concerns, and general anxiety."[23]

Can a leader quell the cauldron? No. But they can make it a little less bubbly by identifying the dominant needs at play in individuals and groups and by adapting leadership and communication styles so as to minimize friction and maximize creativity.

Certainty at Work

Former Harvard psychology professor and current spiritual teacher Ram Dass once wrote, "What I've noticed in most of the institutions I've been part of is that for the first few years it's very exciting, and everybody feels

---

[23] Gareth Morgan, *Images of Organization*, 1998, 224.

challenged and at the living edge. Then everybody figures out how to socialize the game, how to appear to be changing and not actually changing and everybody, because they have children and families now, has to get insurance policies… They've got to make the thing stable, and that sort of tempers their way of playing with that chaotic edge and recognizing what is interesting."[24]

What Ram Dass is describing, is the need for certainty. Organizations are created with guts and sweat, determination and innovation. But they run on fear. A person who needs certainty at work is most interested in keeping the status quo, because chaos is terrifying. And, it might result in their kids going hungry and other bad things.

But of course, chaos is where emergence happens. The great irony is, grasping for certainty doesn't make us safe from chaos. It leaves us vulnerable to it.

When we need certainty at work, we blind ourselves to reality. We buffer ourselves from negative feedback. We ignore the true story our data is telling us and invent excuses and rationalizations for troubling results and trends. We seek the same types of information from the same sources. The need for certainty can lead us to hire employees who think like us and act like us and look like us and went to the same school as us and are therefore likely to agree with us. In other words, we hire people who won't rock the boat. And who won't create chaos. We mask this mechanism for achieving certainty as "cultural fit". It's a lie. And it's harmful.

---

[24] https://www.ramdass.org/ram-dass-you-have-only-three-things-to-do-in-this-lifetime/

All of the above lead us to path dependence – self-limiting behaviours based on what's worked in the past, or *the way we've always done things*. When we're path dependent, we rely on the past – processes that worked in the past, ideas and solutions that worked in the past, data and performance indicators that worked in the past, structures that worked in the past and people that worked in the past.

In other words, path dependence produces solutions for yesterday. Or as Morgan and Barden phrase it, "…self-reinforcing bundles of beliefs, assumptions, and behaviors whose nature – and underlying rationale – may no longer be visible and are rarely questioned."[25]

Sounds good and certain doesn't it? What a nice way to fail.

What's a leader to do? Change the conversation.

Change the Perception of Where Risk Lies

One of the most surprising learnings from my Unstuck Project interviews was that many of the entrepreneurs I spoke with claimed to be risk averse. As in, they really dig certainty. So how was it possible that they engaged in behavior – quitting their jobs to go it on their own – that most people would consider very risky? The difference between entrepreneurs and non-entrepreneurs was their perception of where risk lies. An entrepreneur doesn't want to leave their future, much less that of their family, to the executives, board members and stockholders of a large corporation. They perceive that to be very risky. Read

---

[25] Adam Morgan and Mark Barden, *A Beautiful Constraint*, 2015, 38.

anything about the business world – downsizing, plant closures, out-sourcing, automation – and it's easy to see how they come to that conclusion. Entrepreneurs are passionate and creative. But they don't trust the corporate world to allow them to do what needs to be done for their own success. Entrepreneurs would rather take control of their destiny. And that means, starting their own businesses.

Unstuck Leaders who seek to create an entrepreneurial organization must take a cue from the entrepreneur and change the organization's perception of where risk lies. It's not about doubling down on what's worked in the past. The world is changing too rapidly for that.

The conversation becomes:

Remaining static is dangerous.

Embracing chaos is safe.

The Unstuck Leader isn't afraid to talk about change and disruption. But rather than focusing on how the sky is falling, they point to a new way, one that allows the company to move to places where the sky isn't falling.

Focus on Values and Purpose

Where focus goes, energy flows. An Unstuck Leader focuses the organization on growth and contribution. They let it be known that adaptive behaviors are valued and that the only certainty worth anyone's time is the certainty of purpose.

Embrace Failure

Chaos and experimentation will sometimes, even often, result in failure. The Unstuck Leader doesn't focus on wasted resources; they focus on what was learned in the process. When failure becomes a learning opportunity, the organization does better. There's more experimentation and more opportunity for emergence to arise. Organizations that can't tolerate failure don't learn a damn thing.

Recognise and Reward Courage

Courage is the ultimate antidote to the need for certainty. When courage is recognized, valued and rewarded, it will arise more often. And courage is everything. It enables us to tell the truth, to sense and let go of what's ending and to innovate to create something new.

Mean It

There's what you say, and what you do. It's not okay to say stasis is dangerous, only to stifle change-making behaviors. It's not okay to blither on about values, only to ignore them at budget time. It's not okay to say failure is a learning opportunity only to fire the person who fails. It's not okay to tell a team to be courageous, only to hinder their efforts to innovate.

This kind of leadership hypocrisy is weak, and it leads to organizational cynicism, but unfortunately it happens every day. A leader reads something in a business book and tries to implement without really preparing for the impact of their actions. They say they're cool with uncertainty, because they'd like to be cool with it, but they're not. They haven't done the emotional labour.

Don't say it if you don't mean it.

Significance at Work

When we bring our need for significance to work, we can create amazing things. We can communicate a vision, overcome obstacles, take healthy risks, endure hardships and achieve results above and beyond expectations. If, that is, we satisfy this need with work that has significant impact, not by making ourselves significantly important.

Focusing on positive impact is the good way to meet a high need for significance. The other way is through showboating, backstabbing, bullying, lying and cheating. In other words, by being an asshole.

In his 2015 article in *The Atlantic* called "Why it Pays to be a Jerk", Jerry Useem describes some classic asshole-ish significance-generating moves: "Keep your colleagues on edge. Claim credit. Speak first. Put your feet on the table. Withhold approval. Instill fear. Interrupt. Ask for more. And by all means, take the last doughnut. You deserve it."

Philosophy professor Aaron James has a theory about assholes.[26] "The asshole (1) allows himself to enjoy special advantages and does so systematically; (2) does this out of an entrenched sense of entitlement; and (3) is immunized by his sense of entitlement against the complaints of other people."

---

[26] Aaron James, *Assholes: A Theory*, 2012

What a delightful person!

It's an unfortunate fact that assholes often make it to senior leadership positions where they stomp around, making their superiority known to all. And they alienate talented people who leave the organization. And they piss-off customers, costing the organization revenue. And they bend the rules a bit too far, putting the organization at risk.

What's a leader to do?

Don't Hire Assholes

This is easier said than done as many assholes are superficially charming, especially when they want something, i.e. a job, but there are clues, and if you pay careful attention, you can spot them in the job interview.

Do they talk about their superiority? Does everyone love them? Were they the only person who could solve problems in their last job? Was everyone else at their last job substandard? Do they refer to themselves as victims or state that the situation in their last job was unfair? How do they talk about former bosses? Do they blame others for problems or failures?

Do they make you feel, for lack of a better word, icky? Are they overly flattering? Do they almost sound too good to be true? Do they use "negging" or backhanded compliments to make you feel inferior?

If too many of the above are true, think twice about that hire.

Encourage the Right Kind of Significance

Everyone needs to feel significant and that they matter –
not just the assholes. There's nothing wrong with wanting
to have an impact. As long as it's the right kind.

The right kind of significance comes from the same
place the right kind of certainty does. In values and
purpose. The Unstuck Leader is consistent when
discussing company values and purpose and gives
recognition to employees who exemplify the types of
behaviors that are in alignment with them. Cooperation
and contribution are encouraged and rewarded both
publicly and personally. Employees have autonomy, are
given responsibility and have control over the type of
work they do and how they do it. Also, and this is really
important, there is scope for achievement. In other words,
they aren't given thankless or unwinnable tasks.

Zero Tolerance of Assholes

If an asshole or two have managed to slip through your
hiring process, just get rid of them. That may sound harsh,
but there should be no room in your organization for
assholes. Their behavior and attitudes kill creativity,
teamwork, and send coworkers scattering for cover.
Emergence is missed. Opportunity is stifled. And everyone
is miserable.

When a leader gets rid of assholes, they are
communicating their values. They are setting an
expectation and standard of acceptable behavior, even if
the negative behavior produced favorable economic

results (and it often does). Loyalty grows. Cooperation grows. Everyone is relieved.

Love and Connection at Work

It's lovely to feel connected to our coworkers, customers and suppliers, and strong relationships are the foundation of a successful career and a successful business. Unstuck Leaders understand this and encourage comradery and teamwork.

However, social connection must remain professional. When we're overly reliant on work to fulfill the need for love and connection, our decisions can be seriously affected. We may not fire that supplier, or risk upsetting that employee. Or, we can be jealous or fearful when we're not getting the love we feel we need.

Our colleagues don't have to love us. They should be cordial, professional and kind. And that's it. Get your love elsewhere.

Variety at Work

If you ever want to know what happens when a person with a high need for variety is denied it, simply watch a sales person in a long meeting. There's fidgeting, phone checking, joking, sighing and staring out the window. Or, give a creative person a ton of paperwork to fill in every week. Actually, don't do those things, because you will be effectively torturing those people.

Boredom is a major cause of mischief in the workplace. Boredom creates gossip. Boredom creates the extra-long three martini lunch. Boredom leads to dilly-dallying, chit-chatting and not a lot of work getting done. And, it leads to frustration and ultimately, the loss of highly talented employees.

Boredom at work is bad news.

What's a leader to do? For starters, stop asking people with a high need for variety to do boring things.

People who need variety drive people who need certainty insane and vice versa. I get it. Why can't they just suck it up and do their jobs? Because you're asking them to betray themselves, that's why. You're asking them to be someone they're not. And that's painful.

When I was a corporate VP, I had one of the most creative, energetic and effective sales directors I've ever worked with. We'll call him Tony. Tony was an emergence-sniffing, revenue generating all-star who was perfectly in tune with his clients. So in tune, he often addressed their needs before they even knew they had them.

He was awesome, and I thought the world of him, except on the first Tuesday of every month, when I wanted to strangle him. That's because on the morning of the first Tuesday of every month, my team was to present our monthly results to our COO. And she was a stickler. She liked the reports to follow a specific format, and on average, they took about three hours to complete.[27] I'm sure it won't surprise you to learn that Tony wasn't a fan of the reports. Three hours spent doing anything was a

---

[27] We can have a conversation about how well that time was spent in another book.

challenge for him, much less three hours of spreadsheets and bar charts and executive analysis.

Tony was to have his portion of the report to me by end of day Monday, and of course, he never did. He'd work on it at the last possible minute and on the morning of the presentation, it was a slap-dash mess. And he looked as if he'd been drained of every ounce of lifeblood putting it together.

This did not go over well. Each month, my certainty-loving COO implored me to get Tony to do his reports properly, or else she was going to insist on firing him. That's right. She wanted to fire our best sales director because once per month, he hated creating a report. There was no way I was going to fire Tony, so I took a different approach. Rather than forcing him to do something that drained him, I shored him up. I asked a junior analyst to do Tony's report for him. Done and done. Everyone was happy. Tony kept selling, the analyst got some valuable experience and exposure and the COO got her report.

Think about your own organization. Are you torturing your variety seekers?

If you're feeling a hint of irritation as a result of my defense of variety seekers, I get it. They can be crazy-making. The most severe variety seekers can jump from project to project, constantly changing their mind while not focusing on anything in particular. Deadlines slip, work is left undone, and the variety seeker feels a sense of emptiness and dissatisfaction. This kind of variety seeking doesn't have to be a bad thing though. The variety seeker's mind is agile and innovative. Their particular way of thinking leads to ingenious solutions. The Unstuck Leader appeals to the variety seeker's creativity by first focusing them on a single task or project and then asking them to examine, explore, forge new paths and deliver something that's never been done before.

Are you using your variety seekers to their highest potential?

Growth and Contribution at Work

When we bring our needs for growth and contribution to work, great things can happen. We are curious, seek out new challenges, enter a cycle of continuous learning and ensure that our ideas and solutions serve a greater good.

The best companies, those that are able to address disruption with innovation, are packed full of people who prioritize growth and contribution. They make for terrific employees, but they're also high maintenance. When an employee's high need for growth and contribution is not met, he or she will quickly grow dissatisfied. The best of them will leave. Those, who for whatever reason can't leave, will quickly fall into cynicism, complaining frequently and loudly about leadership's inability to innovate. These people become poison.

What's a leader to do?

Create a Learning Organization

In his book *The Fifth Discipline*, Peter Senge describes an organization where, "…people continually expand their capacity to create the results they truly desire, where new and expansive patterns of thinking are nurtured, where collective aspiration is set free and where people are continually learning how to learn together."

The organization itself becomes an act of co-creation. We'll cover that in Chapter 6, but first, we must learn to understand the organization as a whole; the systems within it, the systems within which it exists and the systems which it influences.

EXERCISE: IDENTIFYING THE SIX HUMAN NEEDS IN OTHERS

In your next team meeting, listen carefully. Who in the room is prioritizing which needs?

Hint: Some careers require the prioritization of particular needs and tend to attract people who are already aligned with them. For example, the aviation profession prioritizes certainty. And thank goodness they do. No one wants an uncertain airline pilot. People who choose careers in customer success or human resources, often prioritize love and connection. Those in creative fields by their very nature, prioritize variety. Consultants and freelancers also tend to value the variety they get from working with many clients across several industries.

Watch for internal conflicts.

Sometimes, our chosen careers cause an internal conflict.

Think of the risk-loving accountant who is so bored she struggles to work up the energy to get to the office every day. Or the certainty-loving sales person who lives in a state of constant fear and anxiety over the size of their monthly commission check.

Venture capitalists grapple with their needs for certainty, variety and significance. They love the variety of meeting and working with lots of different entrepreneurs and their companies. And, if they make the right bet, they'll gain a lot of significance as intelligent, successful and very rich investors. But, they're also terrified. Terrified of losing money on a bad bet. Or worse… much, much worse, saying "no" to a company that goes on to become a multi-billion-dollar unicorn. This conflict causes VC's to fall victim to counter-productive behaviors resulting from a weird mix of arrogance and paranoia.

Now that you have a better understanding of your colleagues' needs and motivations, how will you change how you communicate with them? How does it change the kind of projects you will give them? How does it change the teams you'll assign them to?

UNDERSTANDING THE WHOLE

"Structures of which we are unaware hold us prisoner."

– Peter Senge

Introduction to Systems Thinking

If you're an engineer, you're going to love this stuff. If not, you will also love it, but it may take a little time for your love to grow. Stay with me. Because the quality of your leadership (and your life) is in large part determined by the quality of your awareness of the systems at play around you.

Okay. Let's do this.

What the hell are systems? Well, they're the underlying patterns and structures that dictate personal and organizational belief, behavior and ultimately, results. In the knowledge era (as opposed to the industrial era of the past), more than ever, we have to be willing to look at organizations not as machines, taking input and transforming it to output, but as living systems of interconnected people, resources and conditions. In other words, as complex systems.

The thing about complexity is that we can't deconstruct it into component parts. It is whole as it is. Think of a cake.

We can't tell from looking at it that it contains flour and sugar and butter and eggs, and (if we're lucky), cocoa. We don't see the process of measuring and mixing and beating and baking. It's just a cake. It is what it is.[28] And that's complex.

An Airbus A380 jet on the other hand, isn't complex at all. We can break it down into four million parts with 2.5 million part-numbers produced by 1,500 companies from thirty countries around the world.[29] The A380 is very, very complicated, but it's not complex.

When we observe an organization, we can't immediately see the patterns of belief and behavior that make up an organization's results, but we can see the results, for better or worse. I can look at a cake and make all kinds of guesses and assumptions about how it's made. But until I peak in the kitchen, and until I study the processes, the ingredients and the interactions that create a cake, I'll never truly understand it. And if the cake doesn't taste the way I'd like it to, I'll be powerless to improve it.

Okay, enough about cake.

When we lack awareness of the systems at play in our organization, we're essentially flying blind. We're under the illusion that we know what's going on, but we really don't. Our vision is clouded by what we think should be going on, what others tell us is going on and what the tradition and culture of the organization suggests is going on. It's difficult to see through the fog. The key to system thinking is learning to see clearly (even when we don't

---

[28] If cake isn't your thing, others have used mayonnaise to demonstrate complexity: Cilliers, *Complexity and postmodernism: Understanding complex systems*, Routledge, London (1998)

[29] https://www.cnn.com/travel/article/airbus-a380-parts-together/index.html

want to see what's there to be seen). When we see the processes, ingredients and interactions, we can learn to work with them and change them to our advantage. We are free to create the cake of our dreams.

There are two kinds of systems at play in an organization: Maladaptive archetypal systems and Complex adaptive systems.

Maladaptive archetypal systems occur at both an organization-wide *macro* level as well as at the *micro* level of small teams or even individuals. They tend to be built upon long-term, repeating patterns of limiting belief and behaviour that are unnoticed by senior managers. Their insidious nature allows them to become enmeshed in an organization's culture. They're referred to as "the way we do things around here" or "just the way things are". And often, they create results that no one wants. It's as if the entire organization is trapped and unable to break free of the maladaptive patterns the system creates.

Maladaptive archetypal system traps arise when an organization's leaders are willing to sacrifice resilience for stability. In other words, they are the result of over attachment to our old troublesome friends, certainty and significance. These systems create structural inelasticity in organizations. That is to say, when limits are reached, or the environment changes, these organizations are unable to adapt. They become reactive in nature. They run on fear. They develop a habit of reaching into the past, rather than embracing the present and preparing for the future.

Complex adaptive systems, such as I described in Chapter 1 and will discuss more deeply in Chapter 6, are informal. They arise, produce outcomes and then dissipate, often without fanfare. These systems may create chaos, or they may create solutions that defy traditional organizational thinking. Most often, it's a bit of both. They form spontaneously, without input from senior managers to achieve a particular goal. True innovation and resilience aren't possible without these systems and that's why they survive and thrive in today's environment of volatility and connectivity.

The big difference between the two types of systems is that while leaders attached to maladaptive archetypal systems value certainty and significance, those who allow complex adaptive systems to arise, function and dissipate tend to value growth and contribution.

There's a lot going on.

And when we don't understand how these systems are (for better or worse) influencing our organization and its outcomes, our ability to produce the results we want is severely hindered. We're prisoners of our own ignorance. And so events happen – production quality decreases, employee turnover increases, competitors outpace us – and we react to them. The more we react rather than innovate, the more our world happens to us, not for us. Our world becomes one of problems and decline. We are in a contractive state.

Understanding the systems at play in our lives gives us the gift of anticipation. And that changes everything. So, let's take a closer look.

How to Spot a System in Action

Start with the surprises.

When was the last time you were surprised by a result? Perhaps you missed your quarterly target by forty percent. Or maybe you overshot it by thirty percent. Or maybe a product launched nine months late, and no one can say exactly why. Perhaps customer service calls jumped twenty percent. Or there was some kind of kerfuffle in the shipping department.

A stuck leader hates surprises. To them, surprise implies not being fully in control. It implies weakness. It implies fault. Even when the surprise is a positive result, the underlying thought is, *Why didn't I know this would happen?*

We tend to see the world as a series of events. This happened, then another thing happened, then that thing happened. Events are just that – things that happened. Stuck leaders are attached to the event itself and their expectation of what should have happened. It's hard to let go of expectation – and let's face it, the desire to be validated as a good leader / operator / implementor – and to take a good honest look at what really was at play. If we got it wrong, then maybe we're not good enough. Seeing clearly can be a painful process and many would prefer not to do it.

An Unstuck Leader is open to surprise. In fact, the surprise isn't seen so much as a problem, but as an indicator. It's a chance to look beyond the event, to dig deeper and to learn something new. They don't start with *who* is responsible (i.e. to blame) for the surprise result. They start with *why* the surprising result happened. They don't try to mitigate it or justify it or deny it or pass it off as a blip that couldn't have been predicted or prevented. Their natural response is not panic, not avoidance, but curiosity.

Receptivity to surprise is what allows the Unstuck Leader to detect the underlying systems that created the surprising result. The Unstuck Leader is comfortable with not having all the answers and they're able to admit that their initial judgements and predictions were wrong. It's about inquiry, not ego, exploration, not confirmation.

Unstuck Leaders seek to understand the connections between an event affecting a system, the behavior within the system and the structure of the system. To do this, they seek the logic. Rather than looking for reasons things went wrong, they look for why the result achieved, good or bad, makes sense. How is the outcome logical given the processes, ingredients and interactions? In a study of the way leaders detect "self-organized patterns," aka "systems" in their organizations, one participant said, "I have to figure out how to take each of these moments I'm seeing as being perfectly logical, perfectly understandable, perfectly right".[30]

And this is key. The results didn't just magically manifest out of nothing. The results are perfectly logical given the conditions in which they were created. So, ask yourself, "What would have to be true for this result to have been created?". Then you'll be on your way to understanding the processes (workflow, communication lines, organizational culture), ingredients (people and

---

[30] Henning and Dugan, Leaders' Detection of Problematic Self-Organized Patterns in the Workplace, *Complex systems Leadership Theory*, Ed. James Hazy, Jeffrey Goldstein & Benyamin Lichtenstein, p. 402

resources) and interactions (how the processes and ingredients interconnect and the reactions they create).

EXERCISE:

Think of a recent result that surprised you.

What was the behavior that led to the result?

What were the beliefs that led to the result?

How did the behavior arise over time?

Interview participants both internal and external to the organization. Where do they see the logic in the outcome?

Examine data over time. What changed? What remained consistent?

What other events could have affected the outcome?

This is where the system is hiding. And when the outcome is negative, it's usually due to a maladaptive archetypal system trap.

Maladaptive Archetypal System Traps

There are eight to twelve(ish) maladaptive archetypal system traps, depending on who and what you read. They operate at both a macro and micro level, as illustrated by their presence in the behavior of organizations, small teams and individuals. There are common themes running through many, and if left unchecked, some lead to the creation of others. All of them are insidious, working their destructive magic unnoticed. They affect how information flows, how decisions are made and how people interact.

Each maladaptive archetypal system trap has its own special causes and characteristics, but they also seem to have common building blocks; namely delays in feedback loops, a focus on the wrong goals, measurement of the wrong things, and most importantly, attachments to the needs for certainty and significance that prevent us from seeing our situation for what it is. Below, I'll outline the eight maladaptive archetypal system traps that I encounter most often in my practice.

The Buddha said that the art of life is to understand the structure that we're a part of.[31] You personally may not be guilty of perpetuating these systems in your organization, but I guarantee all of them are at play. Recognizing and understanding maladaptive archetypal system traps and how they affect outcomes allows us to work better within them, through them and around them. We're able to remain personally unstuck, even within a stuck

---

[31] I don't have a specific reference for this. It was asserted by spiritual teacher Caroline Myss during her course, *Understanding Your Own Power*, and I liked it, so I used it here. Myss isn't for everyone, but I love the (slightly cranky) way she talks about authentic power.

organization. This makes us much less likely to fall into these traps ourselves. And who knows, our outsider perspective just might help us arrive at a solution for them.

That said, I ask that as you read through the coming section, you remain open to the possibility that you are in fact, perpetuating at least one or two of them.[32] Remember: An Unstuck Leader prioritizes truth over comfort. We can't fix what we won't see.

Fixes that Fail: Are you addicted to firefighting?

Every organization has its fires. You know – emergencies that pop up from time to time requiring our immediate attention. Maybe a product launch has gone off the rails. Or something's broken. Or someone walked out the door at the worst possible moment.

And every organization has its firefighters. Some organizations have a whole team of firefighters and some are made up of nothing but firefighters. For those organizations, firefighting is a part of who they are.

We don't like fires (or at least we say we don't). Fires are scary. They cause chaos, unpredictability and each and every one could very well mean the end of us.

That's why the people who extinguish the fires are organizational superheroes. When the fight is done, and the fire is out, everyone is pumped. Firefighting is thrilling, it's exciting, it's… addictive.

And like most things that are addictive, it ain't good.

---

[32] I'm guessing: Fixes that Fail, Drifting Goals, Success to the Successful, Tragedy of the Commons and/or Escalation.

Because despite the good intensions of our heroic firefighters, nine times out of ten, we're actually making the problem worse. The fire is just a symptom. When we congratulate ourselves for having put out yet another fire, we ignore the underlying structural problem that caused the fire in the first place.

Other examples include patching together a dated back-end system with Band-Aids and bubblegum when in reality, the whole thing needs a rebuild, or increasing marketing budgets and sales targets rather than dealing with poor product quality or moving harassed employees to a new department rather than terminating a predatory manager.

Logic dictates that if your house catches fire on a regular basis, you don't just buy more fire extinguishers. You bring in an electrician to fix the underlying problem – faulty wiring. But for some reason, in organizations and often in our private lives, we don't do this. We keep fighting the fires. And we do it because on some level, it works for us, even though we know it's bad for us.

Here's how it goes.

Let's say there's a new product launching in three weeks. There's a critical element that's not working properly, and the project leader has just quit her job, so she can follow her true passion, base-jumping in Peru. The product can't be late to market. This is a five-alarm fire. And you're the firefighter.

Let's get to work.

First, you ask for and get all the resources you need. The best people, a bigger budget, and a freaking war room from which you can run the entire operation. Okay, it's really just Conference Room B, but for the next three weeks, we're gonna call it the War Room.

Nice.

Next, you get something even better than the war room. You get freedom. You get leeway. You get to run the show the way you've always wanted to. Because it's an emergency after all and we've got to do whatever it takes.

Awesome.

So yeah, you had to cut some corners, and product quality might not be as high as it could or should be, but you can fix that later. And yeah, the internal team wasn't really up to par, I guess the base-jumper wasn't that interested in training her team, so you had to outsource a lot of the work to get it done on time. And yeah, a couple other key projects fell behind because you got all the people and money and the war room, but that's not your problem.

You got the job done. Fire extinguished.

You rock. You're a superhero.

And everybody knows it.

And then, you go back to your regular job. Where it's boring. And you have no autonomy. And you can't really get shit done. You're mortal again.

You know the underlying problem. The product team was ineffective and undertrained. You should tell someone about that. It's a problem that can be solved.

But yet, you don't.

Why? Because you loved the fight.

And soon enough, the problems caused by the last launch – lower quality and outsourcing of expertise – cause new problems and you're off to the fight again.

Fixes that Fail, also known as Firefighting, creates a series of self-perpetuating problems. One fix begets the need for a new fix and so on and so on. The organization retreats into reactive mode. And as a result, it becomes very short-sighted and ultimately unable to anticipate and respond to existential crises.

Such is the life of an addict.

The Fixes that Fail trap is not only the domain of the bored, fearful or power-hungry middle manager. CEOs, VPs and lowly analysts are all equally likely to succumb to it. Fixes that Fail can become ingrained in an organization's culture. It can even become something the organization is proud of. "We're always in trouble, but we always pull through!" Work feels more dynamic. The team more electric.

How Leaders Get Stuck in the Fixes that Fail Trap

So, what's going on? How can we become addicted to something inherently bad?

Well, it all comes down to the six human needs. In Strategic Intervention coaching, we believe that if a behavior meets three or more of our needs, it becomes addictive. Let's see how being a firefighter fulfills our needs.

Certainty: Definitely not. There's nothing comfortable or safe about being a firefighter.

Significance: Yup. The firefighter is the center of everything. People will move mountains to help the firefighter get her job done. She gets the most and the best resources, she gets a freaking war room for God's sake.

And when the fire is out, she's a superhero. And everyone tells her how awesome she is.

Variety: Oh yeah! If your day-job is boring, there's nothing like a little excitement in your life. Anything can happen in a firefight.

Love and Connection: You betcha. There's nothing like the bonding of a team that's fighting a fire. They pull together, work long hours, maybe there's even a little gallows humor to get them through the tough bits. I don't know about you, but I love a little gallows humor.

Growth: Absolutely. Shedding the usual shackles of the organization's bureaucracy to get the job done allows the firefighter to stretch in ways he never could in his normal job. Trial by fire is a powerful thing. And the firefighter comes out the other side stronger than ever.

Contribution: Hello! The firefighter has just saved everyone! The organization will survive to live another day!

That's five out of six. So… pretty damn addictive.

But there's one other element at play. True, the firefighter may enjoy firefighting so much, they never bring the underlying problem to senior leadership's attention, despite seeing it clearly, but what about that leadership? Why do they accept the firefighting scenario? Why do they keep implementing Fixes that Fail?

Well, that brings us back to our old friend certainty. Solving the fundamental underlying problem is hard. And sometimes, it's existential. And that makes us afraid. So we seek the comfort and immediacy of Fixes that Fail. Just like an addict reaching for a drink, a needle, a donut, a credit card or a warm body.

This is a failure of leadership.

What Leaders Can Do About Fixes that Fail

Step 1: If you're a leader of a firefighting organization, the first thing you must do is admit you have a problem. Any 12-Step Program alum can tell you this.

Step 2: Put some firefighters to work. But save your best people for the fundamental problem. They'll be happy and engaged while working on it.

Step 3: Solve the fundamental problem. What is the common factor in all of these fires? Where are you lacking expertise? Where are you under resourcing? Where are you creating unrealistic expectations? Where are you focusing? What are you measuring? What are you avoiding? And of course, where are the surprises, and what are they an indication of?

Step 4: Commit to avoiding future firefighting situations. In other words, stay on the wagon.

Shifting the Burden: *Have you abdicated your leadership responsibility?*

Let's say you're the CEO of the same company we talked about in the Fixes that Fail example. You nearly missed a product deadline, but an awesome firefighter stepped in to save the day. As you'll remember, there was an underlying issue that led to nearly missing the launch date – the product team was ineffective and undertrained.

After one or two more near misses, the firefighters are overwhelmed, and the company blows a launch date.

Damn.

Customers are angry. Morale is low. Emotions are high. Fingers are pointing. And the next launch is less than sixty days away. You decide to bring in a consultant to help things go smoothly.

It works! The launch goes without a hitch. Customers are happy. Sure, two of your product managers got their noses out of joint and left the company, but that's okay. They weren't good anyway, and the plan is to continue using the consultant until you replace them.

Only you never seem to find the right product people. And it's so easy to let the consultant continue. Yeah, it costs a lot of money, but it saves a lot of hassle, especially now that your top two developers have left the company as well. The consultant was able to bring in her own team to fill the gap. It seems she has a solution for everything. And, her team is getting better and better with each launch. You're lucky to have found her. The company couldn't launch a product without her. Sometimes you worry that she could get hit by a bus, or worse, drop you for a competitor, but hey, things are working well right now. Why risk changing things?

Guess what?

You've shifted the burden. And in doing so, abdicated your leadership responsibility.

Oops.

Shifting the Burden is what happens when our addiction to Fixes that Fail becomes chronic. A problem arises, and someone moves to solve it. In true Fixes that Fail fashion, the quick fix doesn't actually solve the underlying problem. In time, the symptoms become so severe, outside help is sought. The burden of solving the problem is shifted to an outside party (the "intervenor").

For many years, as a strategic consultant, I lived in this space. I was the intervenor. Essentially, I was organizational heroin. Not a heroine. Heroin.

Think of it this way: when an addict doesn't want to deal with the harsh reality of feelings of loneliness, disconnection and helplessness, they turn to drugs to take the pain away. Same deal with organizations. Only they're trying to avoid structural problems such as ineffective sales teams, underqualified product teams or poor product/market fit.

And, as with any addiction, the organization loses the ability to control how often it turns to the intervenor, severely reducing its capability to solve the problem on its own. In turn, its vulnerability to competitors and other forms of disruption increase. The organization is left in a fragile, reactive, contractive state. It's a junkie. And strategy consultants, outsourcing, and coaches, as well as subsidies, bailouts and protective trade policies are its drugs of choice.

The team doesn't get along? Bring in a team coach. Or better yet, send them on a "team-building" adventure. Never mind your role in their dysfunction.

Sales team producing lackluster results? Outsource the sales function. Never mind that your product quality has been declining for years.

The thing about Shifting the Burden is that the whole thing sounds so very logical. Shifting the Burden seems like a smart strategy because it alleviates the symptom, at least temporarily and often very quickly and efficiently. As systems thinking guru Donella Meadows puts it, shifting the burden is "so easy to sell, so simple to fall for".[33]

Like any addiction, too much shifting the burden leads to feelings of organizational helplessness. We can't fix our own problems. We can't determine our own path. We can't survive without help. Our best employees will choose to use their talent elsewhere. Those left behind will only become more reliant on the intervenor.

I'm not saying you should never outsource. If you're an advertising agency, maybe accounting isn't something you need to worry about on a day to day basis. If you're a furniture maker, maybe it makes sense to outsource sales and marketing to Wayfair. The key is to control your core capabilities and outsource the stuff that will take your focus off of those things.

Nor should leaders completely shun coaches and consultants (and yes, I realize that as a coach, that's a rather self-serving thing for me to say). Take time to find coaches and consultants who see it as their responsibility to intervene in a way that doesn't decrease the organization's capabilities. I seek to leave my clients more capable than before they met me.

At the same time, you as an Unstuck Leader have a responsibility to allow intervention in a way that doesn't decrease competencies.

How? Well, by focusing on the cause, not the symptom. Symptom solutions often create more problems. Gastric bypass surgery helps a food addict lose weight, but in many cases, before long, they turn to alcohol or drugs and

---

[33] Donella H. Meadows, *Thinking in Systems*, Chelsea Green Publishing, 2008

form a new addiction.[34] That's because gastric bypass solves the symptom of being obese. It doesn't solve the cause of that obesity – childhood abuse, disconnection, depression, etc.

Shifting the Burden is essentially the gastric bypass surgery of the business world. It's a symptomatic solution that doesn't address the underlying problem. The organization's capabilities diminish until it not only can't solve the underlying problem, it can't even do its own firefighting. Nor does it want to. Its leaders are completely dependent on the intervenor.

How Leaders Get Stuck in the Shifting the Burden Trap

Once again, certainty and significance are at play. The intervenor makes us feel calm and secure. Someone else has taken responsibility. And, once the organization begins to function better due to the intervention, leaders can take (false) credit for turning things around. All of this happens without the leader having to undertake the risky prospect of identifying and solving the core issues of the organization. It's the easy way out.

What Leaders Can Do About Shifting the Burden

Step 1: Once again, admit you have a problem. Look for signs that you're over reliant on intervening parties to keep your organization viable and operational.

---

[34] Robert Preidt, "Popular weight-loss surgery linked to alcohol problems", *cbsnews.com*, May 18, 2017

Step 2: Rather than rushing to address the symptom, dig deeper. Find the underlying problem.

Step 3: If you hire coaches and consultants, choose ones that are interested in building your capabilities, not securing follow-on work.

Step 4: Shift focus to long-term development of organizational capabilities that truly matter.

Limits to Success: *Are you stunting your own growth?*

Let's say you're the CEO of a Software as a Service (SaaS) startup. The company is growing rapidly, and things feel crazy exciting. You and your senior team are stretched to the limit and everyone is flying by the seat of their pants. Yeah, the team needs development, especially the new managers with little previous experience, and there were a few service outages last month because the company is growing faster than the infrastructure to support it. But the whole idea is to move fast, right? You're doing it! Why get bogged down in the (let's face it, boring) details? Why risk losing momentum?

Limits to Success is incredibly common in the start-up world. The giddiness of initial success along with pressure from board members, venture capitalists and other investors who demand rapid growth at all costs, causes leaders to ignore much needed investment in staff development, infrastructure or internal capacity and capabilities. And this comes to bite those leaders in the ass.

As the company continues to grow and the limits of say, an inexperienced and underdeveloped management team, a patched together system architecture, an overburdened customer service department or an inefficient fulfillment process are reached, customer experience will decline. This self-imposed constraint, failure to invest in the things that matter most to customers, will not only keep the company from further growth, it will cause it to shrink as superior alternatives are discovered.

Meanwhile, the fundamental underlying problem is being ignored or misunderstood. As with Fixes that Fail and Shifting the Burden, often it's difficult to see what's causing the limit to growth. So, leaders double down on what's worked in the past. Of course, this only exacerbates the problem. i.e. You can issue yet another promo code, but if product quality is low, you'll only further damage your online reputation scores.

Even more confoundingly, sometimes the Limits to Success have nothing to do with the fundamentals of the business. Sometimes, they're emotional. Employees, or even leaders can be threatened by the pace of growth and seek to stem it. As a scrappy startup becomes more corporate, early employees can feel left behind. They believe that the company is successful because of the things they were doing in the good old days and are reluctant to change now that the company is bigger.

Leaders may want to continue to control every aspect of the business. Unable to let go, they become a bottleneck, as frustrated employees await decisions that can and should be made by lower level managers. Eventually, those employees become frustrated with their own lack of power and autonomy and they leave the company. The leader continues to try to run the whole shebang, to the point of burnout.

The leader, and by default, the company, become stuck in an unhealthy expansive state. And eventually, they pop like an over-stretched balloon.

How Leaders Get Stuck in the Limits to Success Trap

Let's look at the needs at play in Limits to Success.

Certainty: Yes. Overwhelmed leaders who double down on what's worked in the past are clinging to certainty, as are employees who are threatened by the company's growth and seek to stem it or maintain the status quo.

Significance: Oh boy. Significance might be the biggest culprit of all. We become used to the easy success of the early days and believe it's because of our inherent excellence and expect our easy success to continue. We're suckered into believing that we're growing so quickly because we're doing everything right. We don't bother ourselves with infrastructure and capabilities, because we know we'll just keep growing. Early employees believe they're the best and most important employees and refuse to accept new people and strategies.

Love and Connection: A little bit. Especially amongst those who are threatened by the growth of the company. They may find themselves longing for the days when the team was small and close-knit.

Variety: Hell yes. Rapid growth is all so exciting! Who has time to worry about boring things such as fundamental underlying structures?

Growth: Yup. Limits to Success is one of the few cases where an over attachment to a need for growth can be a negative thing. When leaders are stuck in an unhealthy expansive state, they fetishize growth at the expense of long-term viability.

Contribution: I think this one depends. If we believe that our company is making the world a better place, we can also believe that growth at all costs is worth it.

What Leaders Can Do About Limits to Success

Step 1: See the growth for what it is – a good start.

Step 2: Focus not only on continuing growth, but also on the factors that could limit growth in the future. Invest appropriately.

Step 3: Communicate growth strategies clearly and consistently. Don't assume the whole team is on board with your decisions. Be accountable. Recognize and reward those who are committed to the organization's long-term success. Identify those who are unable and/or unwilling to grow with the company and let them go.

Step 4: Let go of centralized control. Don't become a self-created bottleneck. Hire great people and let them do their jobs.

Growth and Underinvestment: Are you shooting yourself in the foot?

Let's say you're the CEO of an e-commerce site that sells customizable dresses. Customers can enter their physical data and receive a made-to-measure dress. They can also raise or lower the hemline, change the neckline and add or subtract hidden pockets.[35]

Your dresses become very popular during prom season and sales triple, seemingly overnight. Yay! Your sewing facility is pushed to the limit. There is a struggle to get all of the orders out in time and truth be told, a few teenagers probably didn't receive their dresses on time. But you figure, it's a blip and once prom season is over, sales will slow down. So, you don't invest in more capacity.

Strangely, the high demand continues into late June and early July, which is a bit late for prom season, but you still don't invest. What would be the point? New facilities are expensive, and leases are long and after all, it's only a blip. And so more and more orders go out late. And by August, you've amassed a number of negative reviews from angry customers complaining that their orders were late, and they weren't able to wear their customized dress as planned to a wedding, shower or bachelorette party.

Oh, you realize! It wasn't a blip! The increased demand wasn't due to proms, it was from a new customer group – wedding attendees. But by now, it's too late. The negative reviews have caused demand to plummet. If things don't

---

[35] Why someone would ever want to remove pockets is beyond me. Pockets, as any woman can tell you, are awesome.

improve, soon you'll have to lay off some sewers. That's when you realize – you've shot yourself in the foot.

As you may have already surmised, Growth and Underinvestment is a special case of Limits to Success. And a weird one at that. A company fails to invest in new capacity because it believes its success is only temporary. It's kind of like organizational low self-esteem. And, it becomes a self-fulfilling prophecy. Performance decreases due to lack of investment, and eventually, so does demand.

Growth and Underinvestment is particularly tricky because its remedy is often counter-intuitive. In the case above, not enough sewing capacity led to a decrease in demand. Are you then willing to invest, even when facing decline? Boards and investors don't always love this strategy. But investment could lead to a successful season of selling holiday dresses, which could lead to more prom success and more wedding success, and so on. Breaking out of the underinvestment trap takes enormous courage and belief in your product and your data.

How Leaders Get Stuck in the Growth and Underinvestment Trap

Let's look at the needs at play.

Certainty: For sure. Often, Growth and Underinvestment is caused by fear due to the memory of past failures. Investing is risky. And if mistakes were made in the past, leaders become even more risk averse.

Significance: Definitely. No one wants to be the idiot who overinvests because of a blip.

What Leaders Can Do About Growth and Underinvestment

Step 1: Take a hard look at yourself. Are you enabling a culture that seeks truth?

Step 2: Take a hard look at your data. What's driving demand? Who are your customers? What do they really want? And when do they want it? Where are your bottlenecks? Believe what you see.

Step 3: Determine where there are delays in feedback loops. Why is there a gap between increased demand and increased capacity? Often, growth and underinvestment results in a cycle of up and down patterns in customer demand. Delayed investment causes demand to decrease, followed by an increase once the investment is made, followed by another decrease due to underinvestment during the next growth phase.

Step 4: Bite the bullet. Invest where necessary.

Drifting Goals: *Are you a boiled frog?*

Let's say you're still the CEO of the e-commerce company in the Growth and Underinvestment case study. And let's say that sadly, you chose not to invest in increased capacity at the end of wedding season. A new competitor emerged and has been scooping up your customer base for the past three years. Sales have continued to decline. In late November, you and your executive team meet to set the strategy for next year. There's the stench of defeat in the air. There's some discussion of how to beat the competitor, but most of the discussion is around targets. Should the targets be increased? The new competitor seems pretty unstoppable – they've been winning for three years after all. What if we don't make our targets? The team's already pretty demoralized. Besides, many of us have kids in private schools and hefty mortgages. We can't risk not making our bonuses. You decide to base your targets on last year's poor performance. Maybe you can hold the fort.

Drifting Goals is what happens when saving face (i.e. comfort) becomes more important than truth.

It starts with what we believe is a temporary downturn. No one panics because we can fix the issue in the long-term. Meanwhile, in the short-term, we decrease our targets. Everyone earns their bonuses, all sense of urgency drops away and the decline persists. Rather than focusing on growth and renewal, we decrease our targets again.

Now we're managing decline. Sometimes, we'll even admit that we're managing decline, and talk about it as a strategy. This makes us feel as if we're doing something – we're not sitting on our asses, we're managing the decline. Somehow doing what leaders are supposed to do – creating growth – has fallen off the table, but never mind. By actively managing the decline, we're earning our bonuses.

Resetting the target is awesome because it fixes the problem immediately, if that is, the problem is managers not getting their annual bonuses (and yes, Drifting Goals is a Fix that Fails – miserably).

Fixing the real problem, the fundamental underlying one, takes time and effort. It's not a sure thing either and therefore, there's lots of scary risk and uncertainty at play. What if we make the wrong decisions and make the problem worse? What if we try everything we can think of, and we still can't right the ship?

So, we base targets on past performance, ensuring that we will be "successful". The irony, right? Well there's more. One of the side effects of the Drifting Goals scam (and yes, if you're a shareholder, this is one hell of a scam), is that all our good, ambitious, dynamic employees will run for the hills. They don't want to manage decline, no matter how big their bonuses are. They want to build and grow things.

We wind up with a nasty self-reinforcing loop – once the good people are gone, it's twice as hard to get out of managing decline mode. So, we lower the targets some more, and the decline persists, little by little.

This is why the Drifting Goals trap is also known as "Boiled Frog Syndrome". If revenue were to decrease 50 percent in six months, everyone would go into emergency mode. But if it decreases 50 percent over six years, you're a boiled frog.

The best example I know of Boiled Frog Syndrome is the newspaper industry where managing decline is unapologetically discussed as a key strategy. U.S. newspaper revenue reached a pinnacle of $49.4 billion in 2005. In 2017, estimated newspaper revenue was $16.5 billion.[36] That's a drop of 77 percent over twelve years.

---

[36] Source: Newspapers Fact Sheet, *Pew Research Center*, June 13, 2018, http://www.journalism.org/fact-sheet/newspapers/

However, the average revenue drop was only 8.7 percent per year. Not great, obviously, but not 77 percent either.

There's a weird sense of "there's nothing we can do" in the newspaper industry. And that's because where focus goes, energy flows. Managing decline has kept newspaper employees focusing on what's not working, rather than on what's possible. The industry is in a contractive state, both psychologically and financially.

The contractive state created by Drifting Goals can become a part of an organization's culture. No one takes targets seriously. No one thinks it's their job to reverse the trend. Good results are seen as temporary blips or lucky breaks, so no one bothers to determine how to duplicate them. Poor results are seen as the way things are. As you can imagine, it's a depressing place to be. It fosters a sense of helplessness. It leads to in-fighting. The company becomes very insular. No one focuses on what's going on outside the company (new technologies, new competitors, new disruptors, new markets), it's all about us, us, us.

Every once in a while, a leader (usually a new one) will try to break out of the Drifting Goals pattern. But in their eagerness to be the hero who turns things around, they set unrealistic timelines and targets for the transformation. This becomes a negative force because the team is constantly failing, even though they're making good progress.

I should mention that the Drifting Goals trap isn't always about revenue initially, but it always leads to decreased revenue over time. Delays in feedback loops means it can take years to reach full impact and that's one of the reasons we so easily become boiled frogs. For example, U.S. newspaper circulation has been in decline since 1986, and newspaper circulation per capita has been in decline since 1946, but revenue didn't begin to decline until 2005.[37] They were in serious trouble, but the alarm bells didn't begin to ring for many years.

Similarly, we may find ourselves accommodating poor performance from our employees rather than holding them to appropriate standards, or we may find that deadlines or launch dates are continuously shifted with little or no repercussions. Product quality may decrease for years before a tipping point is reached where customers become frustrated, and revenue begins to suffer. Same with increasing wait times or declining employee satisfaction.

Drifting Goals are a choice. We may pretend that outside forces are to blame and that things are beyond our control, but the truth is, Drifting Goals are what happens when we choose to look away.

How Leaders Get Stuck in the Drifting Goals Trap

Drifting goals is a drastic case of prioritizing comfort over truth. And of course, when we do that, certainty and significance are at play. Change is risky and scary. Failure can result in not only financial insecurity, but one hell of an ego blow. It's simpler to change the rules of the game in our favor than it is to do the hard work of transformation.

---

[37] Ibid

What Leaders Can Do About Drifting Goals

Step 1: Stop linking goals to past performance. Instead, anchor goals to what's going on outside the company. Redefine the competitive set. Create new benchmarks.

Step 2: Focus on growth and possibilities.

Step 3: Plan for transition. The same old, same old won't do. New ideas, new people, new ways of doing things, new products and services will be required.

Step 4: Create an inspiring vision of where the organization is going. Communicate it constantly and consistently both internally and externally.

Step 5: Be realistic about how long it will take. Set benchmarks for bonuses accordingly. Unrealistic timelines and targets will kill innovation.

This is hard core leadership stuff. It requires us to be aligned with our core values and purpose. We must be expansive, despite the contraction around us.

Success to the Successful: *Are you perpetuating privilege?*

Let's say Bill and Janet are equally qualified product managers who are each given a critical product development project. Bill's team is solid, but their product is breaking new ground for the company, so they experience some early delays as they perfect their technology. Janet's team is building on existing technology and gets off to a quick start. At their first progress report to the board, Janet really shines. Everyone gets super excited about her product.

Soon, Janet hits a snag and requests more resources. Because her product seems to be a winner, they redirect a few developers and a designer from Bill's team to hers. Bill's team was just hitting its stride, but the loss of key members has slowed them down once again.

Janet launches two weeks ahead of schedule. She secures additional marketing dollars to give her product a big push. Bill's progress is steady, and his minimum viable product is testing well with beta customers. His financial models are projecting big numbers in Q4. Meanwhile, Janet's product is already in market, and hitting her targets in Q1. More marketing dollars are directed to her, and away from Bill even though long-term, his product has the potential to be truly disruptive in their industry. By the time Bill launches, there's only enough money for a lackluster marketing effort. No one is excited.

Janet is assigned another important project and knocks it out of the park. Everyone loves Janet. She's learning and improving with each new launch. Bill, not so much. He gets less important work and as a result, his skillset doesn't grow as quickly as Janet's.

Soon, Janet is a far better product manager than Bill, and the contrast is obvious. Bill's disruptive product is killed, and Bill is let go not long after.

Success to the Successful is by far, the system trap I hate the most. It's insidious, systemic and to most people, conveniently invisible. But above all, it's lazy.

In the Success to the Successful trap, those who are successful are granted additional advantages that give them the ability to compete more effectively and therefore win more easily in the future. Sound unfair? Well it is. And it's everywhere.

We see it in education when the amount of funding received by a public school is determined by the amount of property taxes collected in its catchment area. By default, poorer neighborhoods have poorer schools, making it difficult for the kids from those areas to make it into university. Speaking of university, many have "legacy" admissions where the children of alumni are prioritized for admission, regardless of their academic accomplishments.

There are further advantages for children of privileged backgrounds. Research has found that grade inflation is more prevalent in wealthier schools than ones in poor districts.[38] And it makes sense. If your mom is a lawyer who is highly skilled in the arts of influence and negotiation, she's going to have a lot more success when pressuring the teacher than will a mom who works as an accounts payable clerk.

Once out of school, the advantages for wealthier people continue. In their book *The Class Ceiling: Why it Pays to be Privileged*, Daniel Laurison and Sam Friedman show how due to a series of "hidden mechanisms", those who grew up wealthier are better prepared for success in elite professions such as media, architecture and acting. Those from wealthier backgrounds have access to a larger, more

---

[38] "Is grade inflation just another way for privileged kids to get ahead?", *Quartz*, September 20, 2018

influential network for professional advancement, have a better understanding of professional norms and behaviors, and have access to their parents' money to fund their ambitions. If mom and dad are paying your rent, it's a lot easier to take that internship in London or New York that will lead to a more prestigious position down the road.

Success to the Successful isn't just about individuals. We see it in business when companies over invest in cash cows and assign limited time and funds to new innovation. We see it when companies lose interest in new products before they're able to reach materiality to the bottom line. We see it when startups hire the same person over and over again and call it "cultural fit". We saw it in the hiring algorithm developed by Amazon that taught itself that male candidates were better than female candidates.[39]

These policies and practices are developed with the notion that it is smarter to double down on what's already working. It's easy to sell this notion to a board of directors. And it makes us feel comfortable. We don't, after all, want to take our eyes off the ball. But, Success to the Successful can trap us into lackluster performance. We wind up with the same strategies, the same people, the same technology the same measurements and the same tools. We become unimaginative, closed minded and slaves to the past. Those who think differently or approach things in unorthodox ways become disenchanted and demotivated. Opportunities for change and innovation are lost.

---

[39] "Amazon scraps secret AI recruiting tool that showed bias against women", *Reuters*, October 9, 2018

What makes me the craziest about Success to the Successful is the way most people are blind to it. Take a look at your organization. If everyone is the same color or went to the same school, or are of the same gender identity, or the same sexuality or have the same mother tongue, or the same physical abilities, you and your senior leaders (not to mention your HR department) have some thinking to do.

Success to the Successful isn't leadership. It is the very definition of privilege. It is survival of the fittest in action, but it ignores the fact that there was an advantage from the beginning. It's cheating.

How Leaders Get Stuck in the Success to the Successful Trap

Say hello once again to certainty and significance! When we stack the deck in favor of those who are already winning, we can be certain that events will unfold in the way we want them to. That is to say, people like us will continue to succeed. And our world view will continue to be validated.

Same with doubling down on products and strategies that are already working. Cash cows deliver. New products are uncertain.

What Leaders Can Do About Success to the Successful

Step 1: Focus on the environment that created the success, more than, or as well as the characteristics of the successful. Where is there an unfair advantage? Is your core product sucking up all the resources, effectively starving new initiatives? Does your CTO hire developers who are exactly like him or herself?

Step 2: Assess what you're measuring. Are you reinforcing success to the successful? Sure, Janet made faster progress initially, but Bill was creating something disruptive. He needed room to breathe.

Step 3: Embrace doubt. Maybe, just maybe, your world view isn't the only view. Don't take success at face value. Take environment into consideration as well as character.

Step 4: Invest. Ask yourself – why does the system only have one winner? Why can't both Janet and Bill win?

Step 5: Diversify. A team of likeminded people, while very comfortable, is essentially useless. Differences lead to the kind of tension, conflict and debate that create innovation and excellence.

This is why many symphonies audition musicians from behind a screen. Those listening can't tell if the player is a man or a woman. And guess what? The percent of female performers increased from 5 percent in 1970 to 25 percent or more by 1997.[40]

When Samantha Bee was hiring writers for her television show, audition scripts were submitted without personal indicators of gender or race. The result was a team that was 50 percent women and 30 percent people of

---

[40] "How blind auditions help orchestras to eliminate gender bias", *The Guardian*, October 14, 2013

color – a rather unusual mix for a late-night comedy program.[41]

Step 6: Encourage collaboration and crosspollination. The more you and your team are exposed to new ideas and ways of doing things, the better your solutions and innovations will become. Creativity will thrive. Energy will increase. Healthy complex adaptive systems will arise… but I'm getting ahead of myself. We'll talk about those soon.

Tragedy of the Commons: Who's hogging the resources?

Let's say you're a shepherd in Victorian England. Yes, really. Just outside of your village is "the common", a large grassy field where you and the other shepherds graze your sheep. Everyone knows that the best practice, grazing-wise, is to graze until the grass is about four inches high and then move the sheep to other (greener) pastures to allow recovery. Failure to manage the commons properly will result in soil erosion, which leads to less grass the following year. If left unchecked, overgrazing can lead to famine and death of livestock and people. These are dire consequences indeed.

Fellow shepherd Rory, however, doesn't give a shit. Rory grazes and grazes and grazes. Barbara, another shepherd hates what Rory is doing, but nonetheless feels forced to maximize her flock's time in the common, before

---

[41] "The Other Diversity Dividend", *Harvard Business Review*, July-August 2018

his sheep can eat all the grass up. So do Dan, Frank and Margaret. And you feel you have no choice but to do so too. Soon, the pasture is overgrazed, dry, thoroughly and irreparably depleted.

Such is the Tragedy of the Commons. There's a common pool of resources. Everyone acts in their own self-interest. Eventually the pool is drained of its resources and everyone is shit-out-of-luck.

In the twenty-first century, the health of the planet itself is a commons issue, as are offshore tax shelters, unlivable minimum wages and the over prescription of antibiotics.

In organizations, it's often sales forces, marketing departments or software development teams that form the commons. And the same tragedy plays out. Leaders believe that sharing resources is cost effective. But it rarely is. The common resource is soon overwhelmed with requests and in response, they develop some kind of triage system. I once worked with a client who was so overwhelmed, she forced her co-workers to fill out a three-page questionnaire to justify the use of her marketing team's services.

When individual players (often department heads) find their requirements deprioritized, they will claim that their work is an emergency to get it done. Whoever kicks up the biggest stink wins. It becomes survival of the whiniest. Net gains are diminished as the overburdened centralized resource can't do a good job for anyone.

This issue is particularly troublesome for new business divisions within large companies. Writer and innovation consultant Geoffrey Moore writes about how business initiatives tend to fall into three horizons.[42]

Horizon 1: the current business

Horizon 2: products or new businesses with expected ROI in 12 to 36 months

Horizon 3: products or new businesses with expected ROI in 36 to 72 months

You might be inclined to think that H3 businesses are screwed, as far as sharing resources go, but that usually isn't the case. Due to their exploratory nature, H3 businesses tend to be funded from the capital budget, not the operating business budget and generally no sharing is required.

It's H2 that's the sticking point. Even if H2 initiatives are growing rapidly, they may not yet be material to the company's bottom line. H1 managers, not thrilled to be sharing with the new upstart, hoard spare resources by declaring emergencies, throwing their weight around or calling in old favors. H2 managers are put at a disadvantage, garner fewer resources and are ultimately less likely to generate a healthy revenue stream. Eventually, senior managers pull the plug on the H2 venture. If you're detecting a little Success to the Successful here, you're correct. And the results are the same. The organization as a whole is less innovative and

---

[42] Geoffrey A. Moore, *Escape Velocity*, Harper, 2011, 40.

therefore less prepared to meet the challenges of a changing market.

On a broader scale, the notion in Silicon Valley that the only good kind of company is a monopoly (think Amazon, Google, Facebook) also leads to a Tragedy of the Commons. When there's no room for competition between players, and organizations are left to lead entire categories of business, abuse of power is inevitable. Any attempt at competition will be quashed by the monopoly. The monopoly will in time make decisions focused on preserving itself, rather than for the greater good of employees, customers or the community at large.

How Leaders Get Stuck in the Tragedy of the Commons Trap

Certainty and significance are once again the main culprits. We need to be certain that our needs and requirements will be met. And we need the significance that comes from knowing that others won't be getting something that we won't be getting, or that the success of others will not come at a cost to us. We come to believe that we deserve more than our fair share.

The saddest thing about the Tragedy of the Commons is that it has us acting against our own best interests. We are in a contractive state when we act this way. We're reacting to our fears of loss, less and never, and nothing good is built from an attachment to those fears. And, in continuing to deplete the commons, we ensure that we remain contractive. Our fears will become self-fulfilling prophecies.

What Leaders Can Do About the Tragedy of the Commons

Step 1: Learn the game. Who are the biggest abusers of the common resources? How are those in charge of the resources in question managing them? How are you as a leader contributing to the problem?

Step 2: Step out of your own personal ego-system and into the eco-system. That is to say, take a step back and consider the effects of your hoarding actions. Ask the other commons participants to do the same. Show your hoarders how reducing the commons affects everyone.

Step 3: Ensure you're compensating your employees in a way that encourages correct usage of the commons. One way to do this is to compensate H1 managers for performance across all divisions including those in H2. Another is to give everyone a finite share of the resource in question. They will have to conserve because they'll know that if they run out, they run out.

Step 4: Create mechanisms and measurements for how the commons is used. Quotas, allotted hours or cross-charges are ways to do this.

Escalation: Is your insecurity in the driver's seat?

Let's say you own an ice cream shop. All your ice creams are made on site, with recipes handed down through your family for generations. You have sixteen incredible, original flavors that can't be found anywhere else. Then one sunny afternoon in June, you notice a sign in the window of the empty shop across the street. Good God, it's another ice cream shop. Immediately, your heart begins to pound. There just isn't room for two ice cream shops on this street! This shop has been in your family for decades. You cannot be the person to lose it all. You resolve to fight the other shop at all costs.

On the other shop's opening day, you offer half-price cones at your shop. It works! You're winning! Customers are lined up around the block. The next day though, the other shop lowers their price. Easy for them to do, they're selling cheap factory-made ice cream. For you, the price cuts hurt a little more. Nonetheless, you cut your prices again. And so do they. Soon, you're losing money on each cone sold, but it doesn't matter. What matters is beating the other shop. By September, everyone in the neighborhood has gained five pounds and both ice cream shops are out of business. It's universally accepted that you and the other shop owner are a pair of dumbasses.

There's a lyric in the movie *Crazy Heart* that captures escalation perfectly: "It's funny how fallin' feels like flyin' for a little while."

Escalation is contractiveness masquerading as expansiveness. It begins with two parties threatened by each other. Each party is trying to maintain their position through control of the other. In their attempts to gain on the other, there's a process of escalation that reinforces itself, escalating higher and more drastically until everybody feels like a loser.

How does this happen? Well, each side becomes reactive. They overestimate the impact of the other side's actions. Because we're in a contractive state, we instinctively go low (as in lower prices in the case above). This puts us in danger of competing with an inferior adversary on the only variable on which they can win (price in the case above). Meanwhile, we have a vastly superior product that we are now discounting for no reason. And worse, we're elevating the inferior competitor to our level and letting them control the market. Whereas if we were in an expansive state, we'd instinctively go high with positive, real differentiations and messaging (such as high-quality house-made flavors made from old family recipes).

Escalation often arises when a company focuses on a single competitive variable, most often price, but not always, and it becomes a zero-sum game where nobody wins. Often the cost of and focus on the escalation results in decreased quality and benefit to customers, employees and ultimately shareholders and investors. Price wars, promotional wars, outsized advertising budgets, and hefty employee bonuses and salaries are all forms of Escalation.

Escalation isn't only about external competition. It can occur within organizations as well. Think of Jim and Dwight from the American version of *The Office*. Employees, departments or divisions compete for attention, credit and resources (Tragedy of the Commons).

I once spent some time with a group of executives at a large, national retailer that was slow to adopt e-commerce. As I spoke with each party, I came to see that there was an epic internal battle raging over who had control over the home page of the store's website. The marketing department thought it was a place for them to tell stories. The digital department thought it was a place to sell product. In the meantime, a major new competitor was entering the market. Still, the focus was on the internal battle rather than the real challenge before them. Both in-store and online sales suffered.

I worked with another organization where every department head was trying to get at least one other department head fired. The result was a culture of escalating feuding, sabotaging, backstabbing and gossip that permeated the entire organization down to the most junior levels.

In both cases, there was a core reality that was being avoided: an unclear vision and mission. So, when things became uncertain, rather than cooperating, managers sought to solidify their positions, and to gain turf.

That said, Escalation isn't always bad. In fact, it can be an incredible force for good. Think of curing diseases, the space race, the battle to win in green technology. In these cases, escalating competition can bring about better and faster results.

But, if unchecked, Escalation, especially in the tech world, can produce the stuff of nightmares. Think of what could have been the consequences of the arms race of the sixties, seventies and eighties. And then think of potential dangers of hastily and thoughtlessly designed artificial intelligence systems or bio-technology.

How Leaders Get Stuck in the Escalation Trap

Escalation is all about insecurity. And therefore, all about certainty and significance. I must win (to feed my family) and I deserve to win (because I'm better than the other guy and I'm not going to let him be bigger or more successful than me).

But there's something else at play – variety. The thing about space races and curing diseases and even a price war is that they're pretty damn exciting. And, similarly to the firefighting in the Fixes that Fail trap, it provides a nice distraction from other issues.

And finally, love and connection also come into play in escalation, especially if the escalation results in the battle of one team against another. It creates an "us against them" mentality that makes us feel as though we belong to something bigger than ourselves.

What Leaders Can Do About Escalation

Step 1: Take a good honest look. What is the insecurity at the heart of the escalation mentality?

Step 2: Identify the key players in the escalation. This is fairly easy to do with external players, but much trickier with internal ones. Often the players will hide their escalation practices from their bosses. Think of Jim and Dwight from *The Office*. The way to find it is to look for what or who is being threatened.

Step 3: Realign yourself and your organization with your core values and purpose. This will put you back in an expansive state. In an expansive state, we instinctively go high when our competitors go low.

Step 4: Seek long-term advantage on positive differentiators rather than focusing on a single competitive trait such as price. (i.e. brand, product, innovation, service)

Step 5: Communicate a clear vision and purpose for the organization. And then do it again and again until it becomes as innate as breathing to you and to your team.

Your Role in Creating Archetypal Systems Traps

Here's the deal. If these systems are at play in your organization (and they are), then you helped create them and/or you're helping to propagate them. In many ways, they're a reflection of you. Are you a firefighter? Do you tend to escalate things? Do you double down on what's working, ensuring success to the successful? These tendencies of yours become baked into the organization, its culture, its approach to innovation and its response to crisis.

We don't always see our individual impacts on the entire system. We make the best decisions we can, given the information available to us. Economist Herbert Simon calls this "bounded rationality". And it's a bitch. We're wearing blinders. We inoculate ourselves from the surprise of unexpected negative results with rationalization, intellectually dishonest reframing and denial.

I saw this process over and over in my consulting practice. The problem presented by the client is never the real problem. It's the rationalized, reframed version of the problem. Or, the client is in such denial, the problem they hired me to solve was tangential at best, completely unrelated at worst.

Our employees often see the truth clearer than we do. And watching us flail around ignoring the real problems while attempting to solve unimportant ones drives them crazy.

Sharon, an Unstuck Project interviewee, felt the most stuck in her life when she worked for a boss whose combative, scapegoating management style combined with a lack of clear vision created infighting on his executive team. The team hostility grew to a point where even the boss had to admit the organization had become so toxic, it was affecting the bottom line. So, he Shifted the Burden, and brought in a coach. This, by the way, is why I don't do group coaching. There's always an elephant in the room, and everyone knows it but the elephant. Needless to say, the coaching didn't work. The team was unable to communicate honestly with the boss in the room, and the resulting phony discussion only created more tension, more bitterness and more infighting. Sharon, who's a smart cookie, negotiated an exit package.

Our job as Unstuck Leaders is to consciously take the blinders off, even if that means we'll see something we don't want to see. And this is humbling, to say the least. We like to think we're in control of our emotions and that we're self-aware enough to know the impact we're having on others. But the truth is, most of us are in a contractive state at least part of the time. And when we're in a contractive state, we're no longer observers of maladaptive systems and behaviors, we're active participants. Our issues and limitations become the organization's issues and limitations. We are creating the very results we say we don't want.

What Got You Here, Won't Get You There. Take Off the Beret.

You worked hard to get to where you are. You were singularly focused, competitive, results driven and sometimes, uncompromising. You probably broke a few rules. You made unpopular decisions. You did what you had to.

That's how you got here. But now things must change. Now your focus is on organizational values and vision. It's about enabling. It's about growth and contribution.

Writer and Aspen Institute fellow Anand Giridharadas talks about how for many leaders, processing new power can lead to all kinds of mischief. Once we're granted external power, we have to reconcile it with our internal, authentic power. When the leader of a rebel army wins the ultimate battle, he becomes the king and his role changes. He needs to do things differently now. The true danger comes when the rebel doesn't realize he's now king. In Giridharadas's words, "If the guy keeps wearing the beret, beware."[43]

I get it. It's fun to wear the beret. It's fun to be the rebel. It's what made you successful and it's become a part of your identity. But your role is different now. Can you still be rebellious? Of course. Only take care to do it with the

---

[43] You can watch the Google Talk in which Giridharadas says that here: https://youtu.be/d_zt3kGW1NM.

health and welfare of your team, your organization, and your community at heart.

Get Comfortable with Not Knowing

An Unstuck Leader does not have all the answers. But they do have to know how to ask the right questions. Your job isn't to know everything. Your job is to observe. Or as leadership consultant Margaret Wheatly put it in her book *Leadership and the New Science*, you must "sit in the unfamiliar seat of not knowing".

Know-it-alls have nothing to learn. They've been there and done that. And so, they apply the same solutions to the same problems. And they get the same results.

Observers don't jump to conclusions. From their expansive state they are able to step back and watch. They seek patterns. They don't judge. They don't label. This allows the truth to emerge. And from there, they can co-create change.

Stop Asking People to be Team Players

This is a big one for me, so get ready for a bit of a rant.

There're two kinds of team players, and they both suck.

First there's the *Self-Designated Team Player*. These are typically unmotivated, non-courageous people who go-along to get-along. They say things such as, "I knew it was a bad idea, but I supported it because I'm a team player." You see them a lot in politics, corporate meeting rooms and angry mobs. Doing stupid things because everyone else is doing them is, well, stupid. And you don't want stupid people on your team. And if by chance you happen to be a self-designated team player, knock it off. You're better than that.

Next, there's the *Why Can't You Be More of a Team Player? Team Player*. These people tend to be opinionated, non-conformists who are pressured by threatened, authoritative leaders to become team players. Leaders who pressure their team members to be so-called team players do so because they don't like challenge. They don't like debate. They don't like uncertainty. They need to feel the significance of being in charge of a team that always agrees with them. They are unwilling to sacrifice comfort for truth. In other words, leaders who are in a contractive state ask their team members to join them in that contractive state. And these team members become frustrated, angry and eventually demoralized and depressed. You'll recognize them as the guy muttering to himself in the cafeteria line. Or the woman who sits in the boardroom, arms crossed, silently cursing her co-workers.

Because when it comes down to it, when we ask our employees to be team players, we're asking them to lie – to lie to us, to lie to their coworkers and to lie to themselves by denying their own truth, values and beliefs. In this kind of environment, maladaptive systems, which are based on the denial of truth, arise and thrive.

Instead, ask your employees to be *team contributors*. Team contributors, who are awesome by the way, speak up when they see something stupid about to happen. They speak up when they see a great opportunity. They speak up when someone does something great. They reach out when someone is struggling. They are truthful and reliable. In short, they make the team stronger and more effective. They are expansive. And incredibly valuable. And if an organization has enough of them, maladaptive systems cannot survive.

ARCHETYPAL SYSTEMS CASE STUDY

Let's have a look at how the maladaptive archetypal system traps can play out in an organization.

Logan was the CEO of a ten-year-old Software as a Service company. He'd left the corporate world at the age of forty-five to create a business that had since grown to more than two-hundred employees. His company was number one in his category, and more importantly, profitable.

On paper, the company looked pretty damn good.

But in the real word, it was a gong show.

Products were late to market, there was infighting between product groups, customer churn was increasing, and revenue was dropping. Logan was baffled. Why was the company producing results that no one wanted?

So, he did what many a baffled CEO has done before him – he hired a consultant.

The first thing the consultant did, was interview the stakeholders – that is, employees and customers. Overall, he found a general feeling of frustration and overwhelm, both internally and externally. It was obvious that the company's old-fashioned business model was no longer working. It required a large expensive outbound telephone sales force, which was engaged in grinding out dozens of low revenue sales each day. Churn grew as the overworked customer success team was unable to prove a direct link between the money clients were paying and the benefits they were receiving. It became obvious that a new business model, one that was self-service, derived from inbound marketing strategies and based on product effectiveness was needed to revive the company's fortunes. And that's what the consultant recommended.

Logan was reluctant at first. Switching to the new model was a bet-the-business decision, and that was scary. Logan felt a deep attachment to the company. He'd built it from the ground up and survived the great recession of 2008-09 relatively unscathed. The current business model wasn't perfect, but even as revenue shrank, it paid his mortgage, and fed his kids. His wife had quit her corporate job to work there. It wasn't just his family's sole income source; it was his retirement plan too. So, rather than making any big risky moves, he'd been engaging in a series of minor product tweaks that customers ultimately found irrelevant.

To his credit, Logan was ready to move past his fears. He cared deeply about his customers and the people who worked for him. He wanted a happy functioning team and a great product. And when he looked at it objectively, he could see that switching to the new self-serve revenue model was a no-brainer.

The decision was made. A product manager was assigned. Good stuff right?

Nope.

Six months later, nothing had been done. Why? Well, it turns out there were a lot of hidden barriers.

For starters, the company's web-designer and back-end developer were massive bottlenecks on almost every company initiative, be it large or small. Everyone needed them. Marketing needed the designer for the creation of advertisements and onsite promotions. The data director needed the back-end developer to optimize the database for analysis. And of course, the product team needed them both to implement the self-serve revenue model, along with dozens of day-to-day product improvements.

The priorities set by Logan were irrelevant. The web-designer and back-end developer chose for themselves which projects they would work on when. And from their perspective, they had good reason for doing so. The designer took her work very seriously. It not only affected the business's performance, it was seen and judged by others in her field. She refused to "just slap something up". It had to look good because her reputation was at stake. The back-end developer knew that if he didn't take the time to build new products properly, it would cause technical debt in the future. He was a professional and didn't want to "hack-out a quick and dirty solution".

The results were catastrophic. Everyone in the company, including Logan and his newly hired product manager were left begging for time and attention. Much bribing, in the form of snacks and gifts occurred as stakeholders vied to have their projects moved higher up the priority list. Soon, they learned to invent emergency situations to receive resources before their coworkers.

In addition, the VP of Sales realized that the new business model put his job in jeopardy. Once an inbound marketing strategy and self-service were in place, there would be no need for a pricey sales force. He vocalized his concerns at every opportunity and dragged his feet when asked to assist with the transition. Though conflicted,

Logan held steady to his decision to move to the new business model.

The other senior leaders supported Logan's decision, but each of them had their own thoughts about proper implementation. They whispered in his ear at every opportunity. This caused a rift amongst them as well as between them and the VP of Sales, who felt they had betrayed him.

Due to the inability to move her project forward, the product manager Logan hired to spearhead the new business model quit. The web-designer left shortly after, complaining of burnout. Other employees were looking elsewhere as well.

As all this was happening, sales continued to decline, and churn continued to increase. Rather than risk losing more valuable employees, Logan reduced targets so that everyone could make a nice bonus that year.

Logan was stuck. Stucker than he'd ever been before, and he was terrified. His needs for certainty (I need to pay my mortgage and feed my kids) and significance (I built this company from nothing. Who am I if it fails?) were highly activated and, paralyzing. Logan and his entire company fell into a contractive state.

Logan's company, like most companies, was riddled with maladaptive system traps.

Fixes that Fail: Before the consultant came along, rather than committing to solving the real problem of finding a new business model, Logan and his colleagues had been implementing small product tweaks that were ultimately useless to his customers.

Shifting the Burden: Logan hired a consultant to solve the problem for him. Then when it was time to implement, he lacked the commitment and gravitas with his own employees to make it happen. Also, by allowing the web-designer and backend developer to set the priorities of the organization, Logan was shifting the burden of what should have been his job to them as well.

Limits to Success: The highly threatened VP of Sales was actively trying to prevent the new business model from being implemented.

Growth and Underinvestment: Many of the bottleneck issues could have been solved by hiring additional web-designers.

Drifting Goals: As Logan remained paralyzed for several months, revenue continued to fall and customer churn continued to increase. Targets were adjusted down.

Success to the Successful: Prior to the consultant's intervention, Logan had been loyal to the old business model at the expense of the new one that would guarantee the company's success in the future.

Tragedy of the Commons: Constant demands on the web-designer caused her to burn out and eventually leave the company.

Escalation: One of the reasons the web-designer burnt out was employees escalating the urgency of their requests for her time and creativity by declaring emergencies.

See that? All of the maladaptive system traps were active in Logan's company. And, if he didn't address them soon, Logan was in danger of losing everything he'd worked so hard to achieve.

Once Logan was able to step back into the role of observer, he was able to see the systems traps in action. And slowly, one by one, he began to power through the issues they created. Soon both Logan and the company were back in an expansive state and growing rapidly. Eventually, he sold the company at and impressive multiplier.

Yay Logan!

How'd he do it? Well, for starters, he learned to let go...

Chapter 5
STEP THREE
Let Go

This is it. This is where you become a true Unstuck Leader. Remember in Chapter 2 when we talked about how Unstuck Leaders are "watery"? Well it's time to get liquid. For all our talk about values and purpose and maladaptive system traps, none of it matters, and you will remain irretrievably stuck, if you're unable to do this one simple thing: Let. Go.

Letting go seems counter intuitive. Common wisdom dictates that leaders must not let go because letting go is lazy and irresponsible. The leader must maintain control. She must aim for stability. Stability is what makes companies successful over time.

Right? It turns out, not so much.

As we discussed in Chapter 2, the Unstuck Leader's job is to enable complex adaptive systems to emerge, perform and then dissipate in response to organizational issues and opportunities. The thing about complex adaptive systems is that they are by nature unpredictable. And this makes many leaders intensely uncomfortable. So, they grasp for control.

Organizational theorist Gareth Morgan wrote that leaders who are unable to let go are caught in "psychic prisons" that create barriers to innovation and change. He wrote that "People in everyday life are trapped by their incomplete and flawed understanding of reality. They are able to free themselves from that, but many prefer to remain in the dark."[44]

So there you have it. If we're going to get unstuck, we have no choice but to let go. We have to break ourselves out of our psychic prisons.

Let Go of Stability

Stability is enticing because it soothes our need for certainty. When things are stable, we know what's going to happen next, and that gives us confidence.

The problem with stability is that it's rigid. Stuck leaders mistake rigidity for solidity. It feels like solid ground. It feels comfortable. But in reality, rigidity and the false confidence it imbues are dangerous. As any engineer can tell you, the thing about rigidity is that it makes things more fragile and more likely to break.

---

[44] Morgan, G., *Images of Organization*, Newbury Park, CA: Sage Publications Inc, 1986

For an Unstuck Leader, the opposite of stability isn't instability, it's resilience. Resilience is elastic. It bends and expands and contracts. It feels much less comfortable. It's unstable. It's wobbly. And, it's imperative to an organization's ability to survive and thrive in the variable environment of the knowledge era.

Resilience allows for learning-based evolution. It requires integrity, that is to say, a willingness to prioritize truth over comfort. Resilient organizations evolve and diversify – they become more complex. This leaves them better equipped to respond to a complex environment.

The place where we choose to prioritize stability over resilience and comfort over truth, is the place where we hit a plateau. And, it's the place where we get stuck.

Let Go of (Inauthentic) Power

Organizational hierarchies are a good thing because in theory, they allow people at each level to do their jobs better. Rather than worrying about what everyone else is doing, each individual can focus on their specific area and their specific results. In other words, hierarchy allows for specialization and focus. Problems arise when leaders rely on the hierarchy not as a system for getting stuff done, but as a self-perpetuating system for obtaining power and control. In other words, when organizational hierarchies become bureaucratic nightmares.

The bureaucratic model is comforting to those who are not good leaders. And to those who love certainty and have a high need for significance. Their thinking is flawed. I have the position. I have the authority. I'm the leader.

Therefore, I'm worthy. In short, it's for the weak and fearful. The irony of this mindset is that in the bureaucratic model, the authority and power belong to the position (i.e. job title) rather than the person. The person can be replaced, and the bureaucracy will continue to function. Where's the certainty and significance in that? There is none because we're talking about inauthentic power. Authentic power is another thing entirely.

Instead of trying to be at the center of every decision and every activity, the Unstuck Leader enables decisions and activities. They distribute decision making power widely, and encourage diversity of people, experience and viewpoints. This is how good stuff begins to emerge.

In their book *Freedom Inc.*, Authors Brian Carney and Isaac Getz call this process "corporate liberation". According to them, "A liberated company allows employees complete freedom and responsibility to take actions that they – not their managers – decide are best for their company's vision".[45]

It's all about trust and respect. The industrial era led us to increase control and decrease personal autonomy at work. Leaders didn't want creative, self-directed employees, they wanted obedience and uniformity. But in the knowledge era, we need more from our employees. We need them to think, to connect and to innovate. And we just can't regulate those behaviors.

It comes back to the six human needs. Employees perform best and are at their most loyal when their needs for growth and contribution are being met on the job. Top

---

[45] Brian Carney and Isaac Getz, "Give Your Team the Freedom to Do the Work They Think Matters Most", *Harvard Business Review*, September 10, 2018

down control kills that because top down control makes for small jobs. And small jobs make for small people. When employees aren't trusted or respected, negative behaviors such as gossiping, missed workdays and even theft will abound, because we've effectively infantilized them. We've taken away their agency, their creative selves and their desire to excel. There's not much left after that.

According to Gallup's (super depressing) 2017 *State of the American Workplace* report, only 33 percent of U.S. employees are engaged at work. Gallup estimates that actively disengaged employees (those acting out because of their dissatisfaction) cost the U.S. as much as $605 billion each year in lost productivity.

When we let go of control and employees are now able to strive for growth and contribution, well, everything changes. Expect more of them, liberate them, and watch them go. They won't let us down. That same Gallup report reveals that the more engaged an organization's employees are, the better it performs. At the world's best organizations, 70 percent of employees are engaged.

Rather than setting a top-down strategic vision, and the much-dreaded cascading goals that lose all meaning the further down the org chart we go, we must allow change to emerge from within the organization and adapt our behavior and strategies accordingly.

True leadership is sparked by challenge or opportunity and it's practiced in the mobilization of others to solve problems and create new things. This can happen at any level of the organization. The job of the Unstuck Leader is to recognize these informal leaders as they emerge and remove internal and external barriers that may inhibit them from doing what needs to be done. Unstuck Leaders ask employees what they can do to help them do their jobs better. When they identify an issue, the Unstuck Leader doesn't rush into solutions mode, preferring to ask employees what they think should be done.

As we learned in Chapter 3, authentic power is born of personal alignment with our values and purpose and a commitment to growth and contribution. A person who is in alignment doesn't need to control everything. They observe, influence and enable.

We are not in control of our teams. We're in service of them.

Let Go of Message Control

Great leaders won't emerge if they don't know what the hell is going on. There have to be conversations and there has to be transparency so that everyone can understand how their own individual actions affect the larger organization. The more conversations there are, the more learning there will be.

If poor solutions are the norm in your organization, you've got to ask – *What am I keeping from them?*

And then you've got to ask – *What are they keeping from me?*

Don't delude yourself into thinking that because you're in the leadership position, you have better information and therefore a better understanding of the company's challenges and opportunities. You don't. That's just your need for significance talking. In reality, there's more (much more), information at lower levels. And because of that, information sharing has got to be a two-way street. Only through this networked interaction can the real truth emerge.

I've always believed that middle managers are the most undervalued resources an organization has. They have regular contact with people up and down the org chart as well as direct contact with customers and suppliers. They know a lot. And the great ones have a lot of opinions about what it all means.

The Unstuck Leader spends a substantial portion of their day walking and talking. If you haven't had a conversation with anyone below your immediate direct reports this week, you're missing out, because they're full of revelations. You don't know more about your customers than the customer success reps who spend eight hours a day on the phone with them. Nor are you an expert on your code base (unless you wrote it, but even then, it's probably evolved for better or worse). Are you an expert on your supply chain? What about the ins and outs of the daily issues your operations team faces? Nope, you're not. They are. Allow them to surface problems and solutions without hierarchical barriers.

In allowing and enabling information to flow freely and for conversations to occur across all levels and divisions, we're giving up control of our message. And that can have negative consequences – especially if the organization is in difficulty. When my startup company was failing, and our options for future funding were drying up, the last thing I wanted was for my team to know how much trouble we were in. So, I pretended everything was okay right up until the day I had to cut everyone's salary by twenty-five percent. They were shocked and upset and I immediately knew how stupid my decision was (in fact, it's one of my

greatest career regrets). First, it was unfair to keep the
company's failing health from them. Second, had I shared
more with them, the team could have helped me solve the
problem. But no. From my fearful, contractive state, I was
afraid if I let them in on the truth, they'd find other jobs.
Which, of course, they did anyway shortly after I
announced their pay cuts.

    We must stop keeping things from our employees. If
they can't handle the truth, they don't belong in our
organization to begin with.

Let Go of (your covert) Ego

As we discussed in Chapter 2, our ego, aka our high need
for significance, is not our friend. It puts blinders on us
and prevents us from seeing people and situations clearly.
It leads to poor decisions and poor results.

    Unstuck Project interviewee Martin learned this as a
young man. And he learned it the hard way. At the age of
24, Martin had a much-coveted freelance job as a writer for
a large, prestigious newspaper. He was writing 300 pieces
per year, making a lot of money and in his words, he "got
a little cocky". Martin didn't like his editor. No one did
really. The guy was a bully. One day Martin, who'd been
bullied as a kid, snapped and told his editor to go "fuck
himself". He did this in front of everybody else. And it felt
damn good. "I was pretty proud of myself for a couple of
hours," he told me. A few colleagues even called and
congratulated him. Martin felt untouchable. What was the
editor going to do? Stop giving him assignments? Well, as
it turned out, yes. He stopped getting assignments. He

wasn't making any money. And eventually, he left the newspaper. "I lit the only employer I ever knew on fire".

We tend to think of high-ego people as "egomaniacs" – obnoxious, entitled bloviators who bitch and brag and make life miserable for those around them.

But there's a different kind of ego, a covert one that on first glance appears vulnerable, and even the most unassuming and humble of us can get caught up in it from time to time. We can feel overlooked or undervalued. The smallest perceived slight can put us in a terrible mood for the rest of the day, stealing our creativity and rendering us unproductive. And it can lead to stupid, contractive decisions.

Yes, Martin's boss was a bully, and that's not okay. But neither was telling him to go fuck himself in front of a newsroom full of people. There are better ways to deal with a bullying boss, and it should be obvious that one of them is not to tell him to fuck off, but Martin's covert ego got the best of him. Luckily, he was young when he made this mistake.

Martin ended up taking a job as an assistant sports editor at a small-town paper an hour away from his big city job. He put his head down and did all the grunt work, while reminding himself that "this is all a part of the plan to work your way back into the business you talked your way out of." A year and a half later, he received a call from the big city paper's sports editor. "He'd heard I'd been busting my ass. He was impressed. And he asked if I would cover basketball that year."

Martin believes this lesson, where he nearly lost his dream of being a journalist, was the central event in his professional life. "I've been shaped by that experience. I learned about being mature and treating people the right way."

Another form of covert ego-centric behavior is having a really, really big problem. Some of us love nothing more than a big problem that never seems to get solved. These problems not only allow us to procrastinate, hesitate and avoid decisions, but they can also bring us a lot of positive, sympathetic attention. In my tradition of coaching, we call these types of problems *safe problems* and we discussed them in depth in Chapter 3. If we're constantly complaining about an underperforming employee, yet we do nothing about them, we're harboring a safe problem. If we're unhappy with a small product feature, but can't seem to fix it, we've got ourselves a safe problem. I've had consulting clients who hired me under the auspices of solving a (safe) problem, but in practice are more interested in complaining to me about the problem and receiving my sympathy and understanding without really doing anything about it. These are some of my most stuck clients.

What to do about your covert ego?

Start with owning it. This behavior is born of insecurity. You're in a contractive state. Take a step back and do an inventory of your needs, your values and the nagging problems in your life. What fears are at the heart of them? What are you avoiding? How are you making everything about you and your need for significance, rather than focusing on growth and contribution?

Now return to your alignment exercises from Chapter 3. Give yourself the time and space to move from an unhealthy contractive state to a healthy contractive state. Stop. Reevaluate and rejuvenate. It's impossible to be an egomaniac when you're focused on your core values and purpose.

Next, learn to never take anything personally.

Here's why.

In 2008, some researchers at Yale University conducted a study to determine how our unconscious minds affect our perceptions of the world.[46] The researchers gave participants in the study a description of a person to read. Everyone got the same description. After reading, the participants were asked if they liked the person or not. Seems straightforward, but there was a little twist.

When the participants were in the elevator that would take them to the lab, a researcher had in one hand, some papers, and in the other hand, either an iced coffee or a warm coffee. The researcher would ask the participant to hold the coffee for a moment as they wrote down the participant's name and time of participation. The participant would hold the coffee for 10 to 25 seconds. After that, they were escorted to the lab.

If a participant held a warm coffee, they would form a significantly more positive impression of the person they read about. If they held the iced coffee, they formed a significantly more negative impression of the person they read about.

---

[46] Lawrence E. Williams and John A. Bargh, "Experiencing Physical Warmth Promotes Interpersonal Warmth", *Science* 322, 606 (2008)

In this and other studies, it turns out physical warmth or coldness can result in social warmth or coldness.

Why?

Due to a little walnut shaped thingy in your brain called the Human Insula. This little walnut becomes active when you're holding something warm. And it becomes active in the same way, when you're texting people you love. It also becomes active when you hold something cold. And, it becomes active in the same way, when you're thinking about people who have betrayed you.

For some reason, warm and love and cold and dislike are wired together. It works in reverse too. Your body temperature goes up when you feel loved and included. And it goes down when you feel disliked or rejected.

It's hard to imagine that something as insignificant as holding a warm coffee for 10 seconds can change someone's opinion upon meeting you. But it does.

So remember: not everything is about you.

Don Miguel Ruiz, author of *The Four Agreements* says: "Nothing other people do is because of you. It's because of themselves. All people live in their own dream, in their own mind; they are in a completely different world from the one we live in. When we take something personally, we make the assumption that they know what is in our world, and we try to impose our world on their world."

Talk about egomaniac behavior.

And finally, learn to laugh at yourself.

Because you are, I'm sorry to say, a ridiculous human being.

Your body makes rude noises. You get terrible, awful songs stuck in your head for days on end. You tell the same stories over and over. You think of the perfect comeback, an hour too late. You've zoned out in meetings, then baffled the room with a complete non-sequitur when asked your opinion. You've left bizarrely bungled voicemails. You've bounced down the stairs on your ass, tripped on your own feet, slipped, slid and flailed about. As a teenager, you said and did things that make you cringe to this day. And my God, have you ever put your foot in your mouth. Too many times to count.

You're a complete catastrophe.

And that's hilarious.

So, if you're harboring feelings of shame and trauma over your silly, silly self, let me tell you that it's time to get over it. You're one of billions of heartbeats on a blue ball orbiting a midsized star on a minor spiral arm of a run of the mill galaxy.

You're not that big a deal. So, you've just gotta laugh.

Because what's the alternative?

Self-absorption. Self-pity. Self-loathing.

No thanks.

Let Go of Being Right

Sometimes, you will be wrong. And that's okay.

The most damaging thing about ego is how it limits us. It focusses us on the appearance of things rather than the truth and possibility of things. It will have us seeking confirmation and asking for input only from those who already agree with us. It will stifle our creativity. It will keep us on the safe side of controversy. Ironically, in our attempt to make ourselves feel big, we make ourselves smaller and less consequential.

Avi Loeb, chair of Harvard University's astronomy department is kind of a big deal. He has published hundreds of papers and won many prizes. He also believes it's possible that aliens have sent a spaceship to investigate Earth. And he's not afraid to broadcast it. In fact, he published an article about it in a very prestigious astrophysical periodical.

Loeb had several conversations with colleagues about the possibility that the unusually-shaped asteroid Oumuamua (the Hawaiian word for "scout") may in fact, be a UFO. It's flat, kind of sail-shaped, moves much faster than an asteroid should, and passed suspiciously close to Earth. His colleagues agreed that it was indeed, a very peculiar thing, but were reluctant to state their opinions publicly.

"I don't understand that," Loeb told an Israeli newspaper. "Unfortunately, most scientists achieve tenure – and go on tending to their image." He believes this self-limiting behavior is counter to what being a scientist is all about. Scientists should not "…worry about the ego, but about uncovering the truth. Especially after you get tenure."[47]

So yes, Oumuamua may turn out to be just a big, weird rock. Or, it could be the most important scientific discovery of all time. Someone had to say something. Loeb saw no reason it shouldn't be him.

---

[47] "If True, This Could Be One of the Greatest Discoveries in Human History", *Haaretz*, January 16, 2019.

For the record, I hope he's right. But even if he's wrong, he'll be fine. In fact, some leaders are actually energized by being wrong.

Most of us have heard of the confirmation of the existence of the Higgs boson at CERN's Large Hadron Collider (LHC) in 2012. This was a remarkable scientific discovery, but the truth is, in the five years that followed, scientists at the LHC hadn't definitively found any additional sub-atomic particles. Seeing as the LHC was built for the purpose of discovering particles, this wasn't a great result.

The absence of new discoveries at the LHC made lots of people very uncomfortable. Something had to be done. Some theorists wanted more time to continue their existing work in hopes something would appear. Some wanted to build a bigger collider so they could do bigger experiments. But not Cambridge University theoretical physicist David Tong. In a talk at the Royal Institution in 2017, he stated that he wanted "… to go back to the drawing board and start to challenge some of the assumptions and paradigms that we've been holding for the past 30 years."[48]

That's right. He was open to the possibility that the Standard Model (ie. everything we know about physics presented in an equation so elegant, we can fit it on a t-shirt), is wrong. And rather than feeling defeated by this notion, Tong felt "quite energized by the lack of results at the LHC."

---

[48] You can watch David Tong's fascinating Royal Institute talk here: https://youtu.be/zNVQfWC_evg

Tong's peers do not endorse his notion of going back to first principles. They feel that because the Standard Model of physics has been so successful so far, it *has* to be right. Their instinct is to double down. But not Tong. He says, "It feels good to me that everyone was wrong. It's when we're wrong when we start to make progress."

This is the very definition of intellectual humility.

When we're expansive and curious, we're open to possibilities. And one of the possibilities we're open to is that we might be wrong. Intellectual humility is recognizing this fact and allowing ourselves the space to explore our blind spots.

When leaders admit they're wrong, people trust them more, cynicism is reduced, and others feel comfortable admitting when they're wrong too. Problems are surfaced. Decisions are better. The likelihood of stuckness decreases.

Think about your own career. What have you left unsaid, unexplored and undiscovered because you were afraid of how it would make you look? How might your career have unfolded differently if you'd released your fear of appearing stupid or silly or fantastical?

Let Go of What's Ending

Everything ends. It just does. So let go.

Failure to let go of what's ending is one of the most common reasons for stuckness. When we look to the past, we turn our back on our future, on potential and on possibilities.

In Systems Leadership thinking, it's often mentioned that the Indo-European root of "to lead" is "leith". It means "go forth", to "cross a threshold" or "to die". We must let old ideas, old processes and old ways of being die. Because without their death, there can be no rebirth.

And yet, endings are hard.

Letting things end messes with our sense of certainty. We like knowing what's going to happen tomorrow, and endings make that impossible. Endings create instability. And, endings play on our fears of losing significance. I'm important now, but who will I be in the new reality?

But beyond the usual suspects of certainty and significance, there's something else at work when it comes to failure to let go – the myth of the good fight and the noble fighter. We're taught from a very young age that true heroes never, ever give up. They entrench! They double down! They certainly don't quit. Quitters never win. There's always a way. You just have to want it enough. There are no obstacles, only obstacle illusions.[49]

Of course, we shouldn't give up easily. And sometimes, you have to dig deep and fight the fight. But also, sometimes you have to cut bait.

Because when we refuse to let go of what's ending, of the past, of what's not working, we're choosing comfort over truth. And in doing so, we hinder our own as well as our organization's evolution. We fail to adapt. And soon, the very death we're trying to prevent becomes inevitable.

Another reason we fail to let go is the sunk cost fallacy. You know the thinking – we've invested so much time, money, thought, and emotional labour into this thing, we can't stop now. Sure we can. All we have to do is leave

---

[49] Early in my career, I spouted that last one all the time. It's a wonder no one slapped me upside the head.

those things in the past where they belong. They have no bearing on our future decision-making. How could they? They're done.

Unstuck Project interviewee, Mateo, was the founder and CEO of a successful inbound marketing agency. Over four years, he built his company to twenty employees. He had dozens of clients and was pitching new ones each and every week. On paper, he looked pretty successful, but in reality, he was growing increasingly dissatisfied with the company. He felt they were chasing too many clients, grinding out cookie cutter solutions and offering no real value – at least no value that wasn't easily duplicated by another player in the market, and perhaps at a lower cost. When Mateo started the agency, there weren't a lot of inbound marketers around. Now there were plenty. What made him successful early on was coming to an end.

"I knew that the agency's value prop was knowledge. If you're running behind clients, you're not serving them. We had to add more value," Mateo told me.

Mateo recognized that his high volume, chase 'em and charge 'em business model didn't ultimately serve his customers and left his agency vulnerable to cost-cutting competitors. Realizing something had to change, he took his managers on a retreat. There, they made many tough decisions, beginning with releasing a quarter of their current clients.

"It seems counter intuitive," he told me, "but there was hidden cost associated with those clients. They were costing me time, and they sucked up a lot of resources from my team. But it turns out they weren't necessarily profitable. At that retreat, we learned that if we limited our offering, there would be more demand from higher quality clients. Now we only have 12 clients at a time. As long as we're doing activities for our clients that are generating more revenue for them, then their budgets are unlimited."

It wasn't an easy shift. Releasing a quarter of his clients meant laying off a third of his staff. But by focusing on quality of service, rather than the quantity of clients, Meteo's company is now more profitable than it was before the change. The agency is also a more dynamic, interesting place to work for the staff that remain.

The hard truth is, there's always something that's ending.

Sometimes, customer need ends.

We've all heard the story about how no one needed buggy whips after the car was invented. Now, the car industry itself is being disrupted. Millennials are less likely to own a car than previous generations. What's caused this? Outsized student debt, less need for cars as millennials prefer to live in urban locations, the high rents in those urban locations as well as the invention of ride share and car share businesses, which give affordable access to a car on the occasions they're needed.

Very few of us buy clock radios anymore. Or landline phones. Or bar soap. We don't place print classified ads. We don't buy encyclopedias. We don't even buy incandescent light bulbs. And I can't remember the last time someone gave me a business card. These changes were unpredictable and often happened at light speed.

Sometimes, business models end.

The cost savings, massive selection and timely delivery of Amazon and Walmart suffocated the old-school business models of Sears and Toys R Us. Netflix and Hulu will eventually mean the end of bundled cable television packages. The proliferation of shared work spaces such as We Work are threatening the business model of the commercial real estate broker. Dozens of industries will fall to this kind of disruption in the next decade.

Sometimes, business processes end.

Restaurants used to focus on in-house experiences. But now, due to Uber Eats and other home delivery services, they must focus on the transportability of their food. The daily work of a Chief Marketing Officer today would be unrecognizable to a CMO from twenty years ago. If you had said the phrase "growth hacker" to me in the mid-nineties, I would have assumed it had something to do with the maintenance of trees.

In fact, automation and AI will affect the business processes of virtually every industry and every job category from healthcare to manufacturing to agriculture, entertainment, finance, energy and beyond. A 2017 report by the McKinsey Global Institute found that about 60 percent of all occupations have at least 30 percent of activities that are technically automatable.[50]

---

[50] James Manyika, "Technology, Jobs, and the Future of Work", *McKinsey Global Institute*, May 2017

Sometimes, your job will end.

AI venture capitalist Kai Fu Lee believes that automation could replace up to 40 percent of jobs and that both blue-collar and white-collar jobs will be affected. And even if your job isn't directly affected by automation, it could be affected by the impact automation will have on the economy. In that same 2017 report, McKinsey calculated that "the adaptation of currently demonstrated automation technologies could affect 50 percent of the world economy, or 1.2 billion employees."

It's not all bad news of course, technology will also enable a lot of jobs, but that will be cold comfort to those who are unable to make the shift.

Sometimes, your own enthusiasm for your job, your company and even your profession will end.

Unstuck Project interviewee Alex, a CEO, built his software development company to fifteen employees. Soon, he was getting work from large, multinational marketing and advertising agencies. He and his team enjoyed the work at first, but after ten years, the grind of living up to "crazy" agency standards began to wear on them. "I had fifteen people, most of whom didn't want to do the work that we were doing. I had the weight of these people on me," he said.

Alex knew that what he'd been doing for the past ten years, wasn't going to continue to work. He'd lost the taste for it. So, he made the incredibly brave decision to rebuild his business from scratch. And this time, in a way that would make him happy. Ingeniously, rather than laying off his employees, he transferred his existing clients to the ones who wanted to continue working with them. Those former employees pay him a small percentage of their revenues. He's using that money to buy time for himself as he figures out what's next.

Alex is now in the cocooning stage of the adult lifecycle renewal process we talked about in Chapter 3. He's doing the internal work required to push him back into the high energy go for it stage that allowed him to create his first business.

Sometimes, a part of your life as you know it will end.

Unstuck Project interviewee Michelle was an electrical engineer who worked in product engineering for a large telecommunications company. Her job was to ensure the product shipped. And Michelle was really good at shipping products.

"Engineers are always in the background until there's a problem. Then people see them. Otherwise, they're in the shadows. My job was to stay in the shadows, by making things run smoothly."

To be extra sure things ran smoothly and that she didn't create problems, Michelle took the time to talk to the field engineers. These were the people actually implementing the products she shipped. They told her that her job and all the documents she created for them were "bullshit".

"I was very intrigued," she told me. "I thought, I'll do another strategy. Instead of sitting on my engineering throne, I'll put myself in their shoes. I could then give them something useful and simple to use. Instead of doing my work five times, I could do it once."

And it worked. Soon, she was on the radar of her superiors.

"I had created this network of people who weren't in my department. This is what the managers saw. I was curious about other people and I would stick my nose into their business."

Michelle's managers saw more than a smart, dedicated young engineer with a network of people. They saw a leader. Even if she didn't know she was one yet.

Everything changed for Michelle when her company merged with another large telecommunications company to form one giant, gangly, nearly unmanageable telecommunications company. Teams from each company didn't want to work with their counterparts from the other company. Layoffs began for some. Others were shifted to new jobs without their consent. There was virtually no cooperation. And no chance of launching what was meant to be the new corporation's flagship product – the product that spurred the merger in the first place.

So guess what management did? That's right. They called upon Michelle. They did more than call upon her. They put her in charge of the whole product and the 60 project managers who were attempting to ship it. And Michelle wasn't happy about it. Not one little bit.

"When my manager asked me to take the new job, I was upset that they were breaking something that was working. I was working well in my job with my network."

She attempted to refuse. But they wouldn't hear it.

"They said I would be great. I said, 'No, I'm an engineer!' I was stuck in being an engineer. I was known for my tool belt around campus. I was always either fixing things or breaking things. "I felt betrayed. I felt they wanted me to fail."

Eventually, after much arm twisting, she accepted the challenge. And she learned to let go of her old self. And allow a new identity to emerge.

"The first three months, I had to grieve my engineering life. I had to say goodbye to the old me and awaken new skills. I had to change my costume. I had to wear a dress shirt. My old colleagues felt sorry for me. I had to distance myself from them because they would remind me of my old life."

And at first, it didn't go well.

"I felt stuck right from the beginning. It was intimidating for me, at thirty years old to be in front of many older people saying, 'Listen to me, I have something to suggest.' Teams didn't want to work together. They felt like rivals. They felt their job was on the line and it didn't matter if they worked or didn't work because someone in HR was going to decide something that had nothing to do with their work."

But then it got better. Michelle did what Michelle does best. She talked to them. She became interested in them. She felt empathy towards them and took the time to talk to each person on her team, caring about them and learning about what they needed to get the job done.

"At some point I had to ask my new colleagues for their trust. I felt slowly each week was a small win for me as I won two people over a coffee break talking about the weather or their vacations. I'm a talkative person, I hate having a blank and usually talk about myself to fill it. I'd talk about what I used to do, and people would get interested. And they'd ask questions and it would steer a conversation and create new bonds. I spent endless lunches, coffee breaks, smoking breaks with them discussing things that had nothing to do with work. And soon, I wasn't the enemy anymore."

Michelle shipped the product. And only three weeks past the company's original deadline. But it wasn't until six months later that she realized just what an amazing thing she had done.

"After a year on that project, I was known not for my tool belt, but as a facilitator. I haven't done any technical engineering since. I'm a leader now. This is me."

How do we know what's ending?

It can be tricky. Our need for certainty gets in the way. We want to tell ourselves that everything is the same, will always be the same and is therefore fine. Searching for what's ending is inviting chaos and instability into our lives. But of course, that's an illusion. Understanding what's ending allows us to plan for rebirth. Just as Mateo and Alex and Michelle did. Ignoring what's ending is what will lead chaos and instability.

The hints are everywhere. You only need to notice them.

They're in the changing behavior of your customers. There are hints in their feature requests, their complaints, their apathy, and their churn.

Your employees know what's ending. It's in everything they say and do. It's in the roadblocks they encounter. It's in the customer service challenges they face. It's in the things they say they need to get their jobs done. And it's in their resignation letters.

The hints are in the maladaptive system traps. Why are there so many Fixes that Fail? Is it because the underlying business model no longer works? What is the Limit to Success? Is it due to outmoded business processes? Why are there Eroding Goals? Is it because we fail to acknowledge that our own personal enthusiasm is waning? Why is there Escalation? Is it because emerging automation is causing employees to fear for their jobs?

When we refuse to let go, we turn our backs on possibilities and potential. We're inclined to protect the thing that's dying. And that's a terrible thing. Because something new is emerging. Something is waiting to be born. And together, we can co-create it.

Chapter 6
STEP FOUR
Co-create

Co-creation isn't about rolling up our sleeves and leading a team of creative people. It's about creating an environment where co-creation happens around us, in spite of us, and occasionally, through us. It's about eliminating the separation of planning and doing.

This requires us to grapple once more with our old friends certainty and significance. We like the certainty of knowing we're in charge and we attach ourselves to the notion that because we're in charge, things will unfold as we want them to. And we like the significance of being the person with all the answers and all the authority. This is what many of us are led to believe true leadership is.

But it's all an illusion. We can set all the rules we want, but our employees will figure out how, for good or bad, to break them. When leaders structure for co-creation, they put the conditions in place for the rule breaking to occur in a way that advances the organization's success.

The Nature of Co-creation

It used to be that leaders planned, and workers did. The problem with this delineation is that knowledge and expertise exist in the organization at all levels. It exists in individuals, in small groups of employees, in the organization itself and in professions and industries as a whole.

The majority of knowledge and expertise is actually at the middle and lower levels – the levels where employees have daily connection to customers and suppliers, to the production process, to data and to the impact of competitive actions. In other words, knowledge and expertise exist at the levels where employees are *in the muck*.

The kind of knowledge I'm talking about can be called "tacit" knowledge. It's the stuff we know in our bones after being in a job, industry, field or profession for a long time. It's often intuitive and difficult to articulate.

A good friend of mine, we'll call her Melody, once worked at a small market research firm. Not long into the job, she had a major disagreement with her boss over the results of a telephone survey. Melody doubted the accuracy of the findings. In her words, "the numbers were lying". Early survey returns seemed to be pointing in one direction, but later returns told an opposite story. The about-face was weird and based on her years in the industry, Melody's gut told her that the data wasn't behaving properly. On closer inspection, she discovered that several of the surveys had inconsistencies that indicated they were falsified. And after a little more inspection, she came to realize that her boss had in fact, doctored the results to give the client the answer he was looking for. Melody's boss had underestimated the power of Melody's tacit knowledge. And yes, Melody fixed the data and then quit her job.

Leaders who feel threatened by the tacit knowledge of their employees tend to rely on "articulated" knowledge. This knowledge is specified verbally or in writing and tends to include strategy documents, technical specifications, policy manuals and the like. When we focus exclusively on this knowledge, we can make all the rules we want, but they will be broken, because frankly, our employees know better, even if they haven't explicitly stated how they know better. Underestimate the power of tacit knowledge at your own peril.

The Unstuck Leader structures their organization in such a way so that tacit knowledge is drawn out and extended to the benefit of the organization. When employees comingle and share their tacit knowledge in small groups, or what the late Stockholm School of Economics professor Gunnar Hedlund called "temporary constellations", complex adaptive systems arise. And through them, true innovation and transformation emerges.

And oh boy, does this require leaders to be watery in nature. We must be willing to reexamine all of our assumptions about what leaders do. We must learn to resist imposing our ideas and solutions on organizational problems and conflicts. We must stiffen our backbones and stop relying on so-called "best practices" when issues arise. We must allow and even encourage tension and conflict in and between groups. We must get greedy for the very best talent and be worthy of that talent by holding ourselves to a high level of accountability.

And most importantly, we must embrace exploration and experimentation. Because here's the thing. Most organizations in the knowledge era are simply too complex for any single person or even team of people to fully understand.

But, networks or "temporary constellations" of motivated, empowered employees can arrive at multiple alternatives, discover previously unrecognized issues and opportunities and solve problems with high levels of success. Small ideas grow in sophistication, complexity and effectiveness. Competition between groups speeds the process, and results are arrived at quickly.

What's working is built on. What's not working is discarded.

This organic, intuitive, creative process is called "Emergence".

And it's a beautiful thing.

Emergence

If purpose and mission are the heartbeat of an organization, then emergence is its lifeblood. It flows and nourishes and energizes. And without it, the organization will die. Or at least, it will become very, very stuck.

Unstuck Leaders understand that leadership can emerge anywhere in the organization in the form of positive influence, openness to novelty, and a willingness to cooperate, learn and instigate action. The resulting ideas, innovations, processes and solutions arise without a formal leader telling anyone what to do.

In this way, emergence is a kind of alchemy.

Individuals sense change, challenge or opportunity. Their tacit knowledge and experience provide unique perspectives on what it means and what should be done. They engage with others who then share their tacit knowledge and experience. These multiple perspectives may result in conflict and competing viewpoints. Ideas and information are aggregated, and eventually solutions emerge.

The Unstuck Leader's job is to supply the conditions that will produce emergence and then encourage, coach, remove obstacles and get the hell out of the way.

This is called Generative Leadership.

Generative Leadership

Generative Leadership is simply the act of nurturing healthy complex adaptive systems so emergence can arise.

How do Unstuck Leaders nurture these systems? Well, they structure the organization in a way that optimizes the conditions for them. And before they do the structuring, they dedicate a substantial amount of their time to listening, observing and connecting both inside the organization and externally.

Through this work, a vision and mission for the organization arises. The Unstuck Leader does not impose this vision, it is the product of what they are seeing and hearing. When they communicate the vision, it's not through a mission statement or a PowerPoint presentation, but through exceptional storytelling, and by being a walking, talking embodiment of everything the organization can be.

The Unstuck Leader becomes a catalyst for action. They ask questions, define problems in new ways and within new contexts. They draw attention to possibilities and present constraints as opportunities. In doing this, the Unstuck Leader "generates" extraordinary cleverness, ingenuity and solutions.

Generation is the opposite of stagnation. And it's the opposite of stuck.

Listen and Observe

At the time of our interview, Unstuck Project interviewee Tessa was two weeks away from beginning a new, very high-profile job, but she'd already spent several hours with each of the people on her new team. "I'm trying to uncover where they need me and where they don't," she told me. "My goal is to make them successful. How do I help them be their best?"

What Tessa is describing is "generative listening". In their book *Leading from the Emerging Future*, Scharmer and Kaufer define this kind of listening as, "a space of deep attention that allows an emerging future possibility to land or manifest. It is what great coaches do: They listen deeply in a way that allows you to connect to your emerging future self."[51]

---

[51] Otto Scharmer and Katrin Kaufer, *Leading from the Emerging Future*, 2013, 147

We're not talking about making eye contact and nodding along as someone talks. Neither is this about simply downloading or debating facts, though those things certainly play a part. Nor is it merely about empathy, though that too is critical to the process as the generative listener watches for limiting patterns of belief and behavior that may be influencing the speaker's point of view, as well as their resistance to some ideas and acceptance of others.

Generative listening is about asking questions, good ones, thought provoking ones, at the right time and in the right place. It's also about validation of the speaker. The generative listener shows enthusiasm, focuses intently and offers support, even when hearing unpleasant things. Because it's expansive in nature (the listener is grounded in core values, but has an open heart), the conversation flows without judgement. It's about possibilities, not grasping at the first available solution.

The right questions will lead to ah-ha moments where suddenly, everyone in the room has a deep common understanding that no single individual had before.

Perhaps most importantly, generative listening is about taming what author and coach Michael Bungay Stanier calls the "Advice Monster". He says, "…the Advice Monster leaps out of the darkness and hijacks the conversation." Of course, leaders should give advice sometimes, but only after truly listening for the issue at hand. When the Advice Monster is in charge Bungay Stanier says, "…even though we don't really know what the issue is, or what's going on for the person, we're quite sure we've got the answer she needs".[52]

This is where humility comes into play. A leader must be curious, and this makes them vulnerable because it reveals that he or she doesn't have all the answers. Unstuck Leaders have no interest in knowing more or better than their employees. They look for surprises and then delight in them because that is where the good stuff is happening.

Unstuck Leaders not only involve employees in building the vision and strategy for the organization, they take their cues from them. Employees are encouraged to voice opinions, even if those opinions are in opposition to those of the leader. When gathering information, Unstuck Leaders don't hoard it to themselves for interpretation and action planning, but rather they funnel it to those who are in the best position to derive meaning from it and turn it into strategies and actions.

And, Unstuck Leaders never end the listening and observing process. This isn't a short-term project where the leader travels from cubicle to cubicle chatting with employees only to forget everything the moment they step in the elevator. It's ongoing. It's a way of being and functioning. And, they expand it beyond their usual sphere to other divisions, other companies, other industries and to customers and suppliers.

---

[52] Michael Bungay Stanier, *The Coaching Habit: Say Less, Ask More & Change the Way You Lead Forever*, p.60, Box of Crayons Press, 2016. This is an awesome book and you should definitely buy it. I use his methodology with nearly all my clients. It's also the only leadership book I've ever read that sums itself up in a haiku. "Talk less and ask more./ Your advice is not as good/ As you think it is." So, here's a haiku for this book: Align. Understand./ Let go. Co-create. Say yes./ Get and stay unstuck.

When was the last time you spoke to a customer? Or a supplier? Or a lower level employee? It should be a daily occurrence. Leverage every interaction in your quest for information and insights. You will find talent and (tacit) knowledge you never knew was there. Little hairs on the back of your neck will tingle as you sense both danger and opportunities.

It's like magic.

Emerging Vision

Most of us believe that great leaders set the vision for their company. That's what makes them great. Great leader, great vision, great company.

An Unstuck Leader doesn't so much *set* the vision for the organization as they *derive* it from generative listening. And then, most importantly, they *embody* it.

The idea that vision can only come from the top of the organization is incredibly damaging. Not only is it at the core of the Heroes and Scapegoats lie we discussed in Chapter 2, it's disempowering to lower and middle level employees. It implies they lack their own personal vision and must therefore be handed one. When in fact, these employees have tremendous vision that they apply to their jobs each and every day.

And never forget, while senior leaders are busy strategizing, middle management is where everything actually happens. Middle managers see it all, from top to bottom, inside and out. Ignore them, and you'll lose out on a wealth of information. Line leaders, those in production and sales, have the best understanding of an organization's most immediate needs, because they have daily customer or supplier contact. Network leaders, those working in support functions such as marketing, finance or legal, frequently work across divisions of the organization. They have many diverse relationships and the best view of the organization as a whole. They know how to make things happen, and who is best qualified to get the job done.

Generative listening with these and other groups will enable us to begin to make sense of where the opportunities are emerging. From this, we may derive a company vision.

A good vision must pull us forward, toward something bigger than ourselves. Record revenues is not a vision. Neither is a low churn rate or high employee satisfaction. These are indicators.

The vision should be about the external impact of the organization. Making life better for people, empowering people and connecting people are the building blocks of a vision.

See that? Low churn rates don't get most of us out of bed in the morning. It has to be bigger. It has to connect. Or as system leadership guru Peter Senge says, "It's not what the vision is, it's what the vision does."[53]

To do great things, the vision must come from a place of truth, not comfort. Most importantly, it must focus the organization on what it could be, not what it should be. In other words, it must be expansive in nature.

Co-creation begins with the belief that at its core, what the company is trying to achieve is deeply important. But the greatest vision in the world is useless if we can't

---

[53] Peter M. Senge, *The Fifth Discipline*, Crown Business, New York, 2006, p.143

communicate it effectively. And to do that, we have to show up.

Show Up

Unstuck Leaders know how to show up. They don't scurry around the office, head down, wrapped up in themselves, their fears and their woes. They're not constantly looking at their phones. They're present. And, they're aware of their *affective presence*, that is, the way they make others feel when around them.

A study about the affective presence of leaders found that a positive leader was linked to better team information sharing which led to better team innovation.[54] I can well believe it. I once had a boss who would light up whenever an employee stepped into his office. "Ms. Sims! And how are you today? Let's get to work!" His positivity made me feel validated, and as a result, I was more energetic and confident when presenting ideas, and more open when he challenged them. In his presence, I arrived at more effective solutions. He made me better at my job.

It's all about how you show up.

I was training a group of new leaders recently, and at the beginning of our session together, I asked each of them to describe how they showed up for work that morning. They gave me a mix of stressed, annoyed, happy and enthusiastic. In several cases, what had happened on their commute played a part in how they showed up. Subway delays – annoyed. Flying through a series of green lights –

---

[54] Madrid, H.P., Totterdell, P., Niven, K. et al, 2016, "Leader Affective Presence and Innovation in Teams". *Journal of Applied Psychology.*

happy. But the thing is, their employees didn't know about the subway or the green lights. They did, however, feel the energy those situations created. And in the case of the bad commuting experiences, the day was off to a poor start (energetically speaking), for absolutely no reason.

Something else happened in that training session. Four of the seven participants mentioned that on their way into the office, they ran into a woman we'll call Quinn. Each of them lit up when talking about Quinn, and how fantastic it was to run into her that morning. One of them even said "Lucky me, I got to take the elevator with Quinn. I couldn't be cranky with her next to me."

So, who was Quinn?

The receptionist. An extraordinarily cheerful, positive, kind and empathetic receptionist. Consider the power that Quinn had in that organization. People wanted to be around her because they felt good in her presence. It's easy to see the knock-on effect of this. Who wouldn't go out of their way to help Quinn if she needed it? Who wouldn't recommend her for a promotion? Who wouldn't want to be on her team?

I would venture that Quinn was very aware of her affect and its effect on others. Affective presence is a skill that can be practiced. It's about finding the positive in bad situations. It's about regulating emotional blips such as frustration, fear, sadness and even excitement (which can really freak people out, if over the top). At its core, affective presence is about creating a space between feeling and acting. It's about maturity.

Another way Unstuck Leaders show up is by using storytelling as a way to communicate the values, purpose and vision of the organization. Behaviors that are aligned with the vision are encouraged and publicly acknowledged. When an event happens – a target is hit or missed, a new product is launched, a new budget is formed – the story is told through the filter of the vision.

When affective presence and storytelling are practiced consistently, a leader can become the very embodiment of the company's vision. When we think of this kind of leader, we may think of Arianna Huffington or Richard Branson. But a chef, or a fashion designer or an editor-in-chief can also embody a vision. So can a retail manager.

My first boss was an 18-year-old store manager of a Canadian fashion chain called Suzy Shier. She loved her shop. She wore the clothes.[55] She never missed a Saturday and in the six weeks leading up to Christmas, she didn't take a day off at all. She treated her customers as old friends and never let anyone leave the store with something that was unflattering. That was just a matter of principle. She called her employees "Suzy girls". Her Suzy girls had a way of doing things and she made damn sure we did them. Though she was just one store manager in a chain of hundreds, she embodied the vision of the company so well, to us, she *was* Suzy Shier.

Think of this as the *Be the Change you want to See* philosophy of leadership. When we show up with passion, integrity and authenticity, we become walking, talking symbols of our vision.

A new shared meaning emerges.

And so do new possibilities.

---

[55] It was the eighties, so think bright, acrylic and shoulder pads.

Structure for Emergence

At its simplest, we want to create an environment where people are not just allowed, but eager to talk to each other. An environment where they understand what each other do, what they're working on, where there's success and where there's challenge. There must be trust so that people are willing and able to talk and there must be transparency so that everyone is working with the same data and knowledge.

The Unstuck Leader's instinct is to combine things (people, resources, products and processes) rather than separate them. Cross-pollination is how the alchemy of emergence becomes possible. This can be done in formal ways through the creation of an innovation team, but we must also allow "temporary constellations" of people to happen. We can't become threatened by the lack of control this kind of structure implies.

The Unstuck Leader isn't caught up in the formalities of status and position. They encourage lateral communication. It's okay to talk directly to someone in another division. There's no need to go up the chain of command.

The Unstuck Leader protects those who are innovating from the kinds of things that slow down innovation such as overly cautious legal departments, controlling HR departments or an uncompromising head of finance. At the same time, they move resources such as sales talent, money and physical space to accommodate the innovators and give them every possibility of success.

The Unstuck Leader keeps a close eye on what's working and what isn't. If an experiment is failing, it will be quickly discontinued. No zombie projects are tolerated as they not only waste time and resources, they cause disillusionment for both those on the innovation team and those watching from other teams.[56] If it failed, it failed. Learn what we can, celebrate the effort and then move on.

Of course, all of this causes tension and conflict. The Unstuck Leader gives up the need to get in the middle of that tension and conflict. They'll seek out and solve for any maladaptive system traps, but they won't get in the way of creative differences. They might act as a coach, but not as a police officer or worse, a judge.

That's because tension is good. And conflict is great.

Tension is Good

My client Gilda is a dynamic, entrepreneurial, get 'er done kind of woman. I think she's awesome. Anyway, Gilda was recently offered a job in a new city and she was pretty excited about it. The job was in a new industry and the company was looking to expand nationally over the next five years. Gilda would be playing a key role in the expansion process. Her first week at the new job was lovely. Her boss was laid back and kind, unlike the boss she had left back home. Her new coworkers were very sweet and welcoming. The place totally lacked drama. Gilda felt like she could breathe for the first time in years. She was excited to get to work and we agreed to put her

---

[56] Zombie projects are those that have obviously failed and are essentially dead, but for some reason, continue to operate as if they were alive.

coaching sessions on a brief hiatus while she got herself settled.

Three months later, we reconnected. I had been excited to hear about all the great things Gilda was doing at her new company, but she told me a very different story. She was bored off her ass, frustrated, annoyed and ready to quit. "I feel less challenged than I've felt in any job," she told me.

It turns out, the organization was so nice, nothing ever got done. "There's lots of twiddling of thumbs waiting for things to fall into place. I'm having a hard time cooking things up to get me excited. When I come up with new project ideas, the team is like, 'Oh, no thanks, we're good'."

Not only are the company's plans for national expansion going nowhere, an excellent employee like Gilda, who they spent a lot of effort hiring, and money relocating is so frustrated she's job hunting after only three months.

Why? Because the company is utterly devoid of tension. And that ain't good. If everything is hunky dory all the time, chances are, something is being missed, be it an opportunity or a threat.

The traditional view of leadership is that the presence of tension is a failure. This is an unproductive notion. If there's never any tension, there can be no learning, no growing, and no creativity.

Back when I was a start-up CEO, I had a coffee with a friend, we'll call him Ben, who himself was a former CEO of not one, but two start-ups. At the time of our meeting though, Ben had left the high-pressure life of a CEO and was the director of a start-up incubator – a nice, but uneventful job. He asked how I was, and I found myself venting about being jerked around by potential investors, my inability to retain a talented designer, my frustrating failure to get the results I wanted and my complete and utter lack of sleep. Ben's response? Well, his eyes lit up and he said, "Oh wow, you're really making me miss the game!" Ben knew he was at his best when he had some tension in his life. Not long after our coffee, he left the incubator and launched a venture capital fund.

To tolerate tension and reap its rewards, we must learn to live with the discomfort it creates. That's right, we have to manage our need for certainty by focusing not on the discomfort, but on the exploration ahead. We don't know how things will turn out. We don't know if we can solve the problem, launch the product, build the team, or write the algorithm, but we know where we want to go.

It's our job as leaders to create tension, embrace it and sustain it. "Oh, no thanks, we're good," must never be uttered. Instead, we must highlight the gap between where we are and where we want to be.

Tension is born of truth and it creates energy. When we make space for it, and we act, analyze and make decisions from that place of truth, fantastic things are created.

That said, all this creative tension doesn't mean you and your team have to live in a permanent state of agonizing angst. That's ridiculous. It's true, your need for certainty will be screaming, but if the conditions are right, you will also be very present, focused and in the moment.

I, like Ben, often look back at stressful and anxious times with fondness and nostalgia. In those moments, I was operating at full capacity. I was creative and inventive. I was energized and excited. We become our best selves in our moments of greatest challenge.

Conflict is Great

Where tension is felt personally, conflict is experienced between two or more parties. It's the result of a clash of ideas, cultural norms and passions. And, like tension, it's essential to the growth, evolution and renewal of the organization. Without healthy conflict, an organization will stagnate.

Am I saying we want everyone at each other's throats? Of course not. Conflict doesn't always have to be fireworks. But I would argue that it's only unhealthy conflict that is problematic. Unhealthy conflict is the kind where the conversation quickly devolves to who is stupid and who is evil.

Healthy conflict is another thing entirely. It's about discussion and debate. It's about drawing out tacit knowledge. It's about surfacing previously unseen issues and opportunities. It's about creating a shared understanding. And it's about creating the best possible solutions.

The key to healthy conflict is creating conditions where employees don't freak out when there's disagreement. Conflict is expected. Embrace it. This allows personalities and personal bugaboos to settle and for constructive communication and learning to occur.

Unstuck Leaders make it clear that we're looking for a solution, not making each other right or wrong. Organizational focus is shifted to calmly working the problem and it's made clear that there will be no negative outcome for expressing oneself. There are also firm rules of engagement predicated on mutual respect.

Because here's the truth. Conflict is not episodic. It doesn't simply erupt out of nowhere and then dissipate. It's always there. The Unstuck Leader knows how to put it to use.

Using Tension and Conflict

Start with tension. It's pretty easy to create; simply ask a question, a good one, aimed at improving the long-term competency or competitiveness of the organization. University of Toronto business professors Jennifer Riel and Roger Martin have a very simple format for the question. They recommend using "How might we…"[57]

How might we…

- Make more of that thing?

- Do that thing faster?

- Sell more of those things?

- Do something no one has ever done before?

---

[57] Jennifer Riel and Roger Martin, *Creating Great Choices, A Leaders Guide to Integrative Thinking*, 2017, HBR Press.

It's imperative to make the question really, really tough. For example, a blood bank may ask the question: How can we increase our number of O-negative-type donors by 100 percent?

If your organization is staffed with normal human beings, a really, really tough question will create a lot of tension. That's good. Well done.

Now that we have a good question, there are two methodologies I like to use to answer it: *We can, if...* and *Integrative Thinking*. Let's take a closer look at each.

We can, if...

First, let's communicate the question in a way that gets everyone really excited about it. We'll do this by focusing on the big juicy outcome.

For the blood bank question above, the juicy outcome could be: If we can increase the number of O-negative-type blood donors by 100 percent, we can save thousands of additional lives this year.[58] Remember, it has to have purpose built in. It has to be bigger than all of us.

Okay, so now we have some real creative tension going. We are here, but the promised land is way over there.

Now we're going to do something counterintuitive. We're going to get the team to list all the reasons our vision is impossible. It will feel a bit like letting the air out of everyone's happy balloon, and yes, it will cause more tension, but stick with me.

---

[58] O-negative blood is relatively rare and can be used in people of all blood types, making it particularly valuable.

This is where conflict arises, as team members will disagree about what's possible and what's not possible. For the optimists on the team, this will feel very uncomfortable. The pessimists though, will love it! Let them debate it out and land on three to five key obstacles that will keep us from meeting our goal.

- People don't like giving blood because they believe (falsely) that it's icky and painful.

- People don't have time to visit a donation center.

- Donors understand they are saving a life, but because the recipient is anonymous, they feel disconnected from the process and are less likely to become repeat donors.

Now that we have clarity on what needs to be solved to make the vision a reality, it's time to answer the "How might we…" question. And to do so, we're going to use a technique from one of my all-time favorite books, *A Beautiful Constraint, How to Transform Your Limitations into Advantages, and Why It's Everyone's Business*[59] by Adam Morgan and Mark Barden.

For each obstacle, we're going to strategize. And then we're going to knock 'em down, one by one. And to do that, we'll use the phrase, "We can, if…".

How might we get 100 percent more O-negative-type people to donate blood?

---

[59] Yup, that's a really long title. Never mind that, you should buy this book. The authors have a way of making anything and everything seem possible.

- We can, if we invest in an advertising campaign to educate potential donors about the relative painlessness of blood donation in a fun and engaging way.

- We can, if we create mobile donation centers that operate out of shopping centers and office buildings.

- We can, if we text donors when their blood is used in a recipient, thus giving them a higher-level reward than just a simple thank you, increasing the likelihood of repeat donations. (This by the way, is how Sweden's blood bank solved the problem – and I think it's genius.)[60]

Watching the obstacles fall is magical. And it leaves the team feeling like dragon slayers. The process is so energizing, soon they'll be on the hunt for more dragons to slay, and more innovations will be co-created. It's a powerful thing.

Integrative Thinking

Let's go back to Professors Riel and Martin. They assert that the traditional model of organizational decision-making, where choices are outlined, weighed and voted

---

[60] Jon Ston, "Blood donors in Sweden get a text message whenever their blood saves someone's life", *The Independent*, June 10, 2015.

upon to determine a preferred solution, is deeply flawed.[61] I think they're right.

In the Integrative Thinking model, rather than mitigating differences to arrive at a consensus, differences are amplified, allowing the team to examine the problem from multiple angles, and to arrive at a truly novel, often groundbreaking solution.

This is achieved by taking the best elements from two opposing (or conflicting) models and combing them to create a third, (integrated) model. Rather than engaging in a series of decision-making tradeoffs that then have to be sold to the rest of the team, the integrated solution is by its nature, agreeable to all participants.

Let's go through an example.

Question: How might we increase our market share by 50 percent?

First, we consider two opposing models for solving the problem. To solve for increasing market share, we may consider product differentiation vs. category consistency. Should we be different than everyone else? Or should we be the same as everyone else?

Then, we map out the benefits of each model and "play with the pathways to integration". That is, we figure out how to take the best of each, to create something new. In this case, we'll be exploring models that increase market share through *both* product differentiation *and* category consistency.

---

[61] I'll give you a barebones view of the Integrative Thinking model here, but you'll want to learn more in Riel and Martin's excellent book, which I referenced earlier in this chapter, as well as Martin's earlier book, *The Opposable Mind*, Harvard Business Press, 2007

We may land on several combinations. There will likely be tension and conflict within the team about which product features should be different, and which should be the same as those of our competitors. And so, we experiment. We test, measure, evaluate, tweak and test again until we arrive at the undisputed best solution.

Integrative Thinking is effective because it uses tension and conflict to help us understand the true nature of the problem.

It's ironic isn't it? In Integrative Thinking, the willingness to engage in tension and conflict early in the process leads to a harmonious solution. We get the best of all worlds. In the traditional model, fear of tension and conflict leads to a more peaceful decision-making process, but ultimately, because of the either / or nature of the voting process, disharmony after the solution is arrived at.

All of this is to say that in an environment where debate, dissent and constructive criticism, i.e. tension and conflict, are normalized, we are freed to generate new ideas, challenge each other and create solutions to problems that once seemed impossible to solve.

But none of this happens without excellent people.

Get Greedy for Talent

Co-creation is about possibilities. We must build our teams in such a way that the greatest number of possibilities arise.

First, the Unstuck Leader needs team members who are intellectually curious, conscientious, openminded, kind, empathetic and above all, courageous. In short, they must be able to live in a world of uncertainty, ambiguity, tension and conflict, and still thrive.

Second, the Unstuck Leader needs a team that is diverse in perspective – from different cultures, backgrounds, ethnicities, sexualities, gender identities, economic classes and physical abilities. I'm not talking about political correctness. I'm talking about maximizing possibility. This is difficult for many leaders, as ironically, it's the times when we need diversity of perspectives the most, i.e. when we're trying to solve problems, that we tend to crave the comfort of being around people who are the most like us. Even when we're not particularly stressed, we may still fail to seek diverse opinions because we have a tendency to think that everyone else thinks the same way we do.

Beyond getting the right talent in the room, we have to be diligent about keeping it in the room. The temporary constellations of problem solvers that arise in complex adaptive systems require a certain level of *know-who* as much as *know-what, know-how* and *know-when*. A group can't come together if they don't know or trust each other. Tacit knowledge cannot grow and be exploited, if no one is ever around long enough to acquire any.

Organizations that design for high employee churn, through overwork, underpay or lack of internal mobility are putting themselves at a terrible disadvantage in the long run. Fresh blood can inject energy into a system temporarily, but long-term commitment of the right kind of employees is far more powerful. When team members know and trust each other, informal networks form, respectful, healthy debate increases, knowledge is shared, solutions are found quicker and are more effective.

The best way to keep the right kind of employees in place isn't through perks and free lunches, it's through leadership accountability.

Be Accountable

We simply must stand for something if we're going to be worthy of the best talent in the world.

Don't say you're going to do the things an Unstuck Leader does if you're not prepared to follow through and to live with the discomfort of doing so. As Unstuck Leaders, our personal integrity can never be in question. We cannot dilute our vision, let our goals drift or allow ourselves to remain mired in maladaptive system traps. Because if we do, we'll create a storm of cynicism in our organization.

Lacking the courage to fulfill our vision is an unforgivable betrayal of the people who trusted us and have given us not just their labor and genius, but also a piece of their souls.

The annual employee satisfaction survey isn't going to cut it. Accountability happens in how we show up every day, in every interaction and every response.

We must give them the certainty of purpose, and the significance of being seen and heard. We must trust them. And must give them the freedom to co-create the future of the organization.

Accountability begins with saying *Yes*.

Chapter 7
STEP FIVE
Say Yes

Unstuck Leadership isn't a specific form of action, or a title or even a state of being. It's a practice. Just as we might have a meditation practice or a professional practice, or perhaps a spiritual practice, the practice of Unstuck Leadership puts us in a constant state of learning and improvement.

Our practice won't make us perfect. We'll get things wrong from time to time. God knows I've gotten it wrong many times. But with each mistake or glitch or imperfection, we learn and commit to doing better next time. And that commitment requires us to say yes. Yes to growth. Yes to change. Yes to responsibility. Yes to our true selves, and yes to what is emerging within us and around us.

Committed practice is hard. Most of us get in our own way. We let negative thoughts seep into our souls, distracting us, sapping our energy and robbing us of our authentic power. In his book, *The War of Art*, writer Steven Pressfield calls this phenomenon "The Resistance". Resistance is the force that keeps us from living the life we want, from taking the risks we should, and from creating the things we are capable of creating. Any time we act against our best interests, it is due to our own inner Resistance.

As Pressfield describes it, "Resistance cannot be seen, touched, heard, or smelled. But it can be felt. We experience it as an energy field radiating from a work-in-potential. It's a repelling force. It's negative. Its aim is to shove us away, distract us, prevent us from doing our work."[62]

Resistance turns up in the form of safe problems that distract us from our real problems, that is to say the quality ones, whose solutions will propel us to a new level of success. It turns up in the maladaptive system traps that steal our energy and potential. It whispers in our ear before we say the controversial thing in the brainstorming session. And, confoundingly, it's most powerful just as we're about to launch, publish, or present.

Allow me to testify. As I'm writing these final pages of this book, I find myself in a spectacular battle with Resistance. I have a pounding headache and am struggling to sit here at my desk. I feel an intense pull toward my sofa, where I'd dearly love to flop down, and watch back-to-back episodes of *Queer Eye* until I fall asleep.

---

[62] Steven Pressfield, *The War of Art*, Black Irish Entertainment, New York, 2003, p. 7

Resistance is a clue. If we're resisting something, it's because it wants to be heard, but we don't want to hear it. We're avoiding it, sweeping it under the rug so that we may remain in hunky dory mode. We're resisting the thing that wants to emerge. And then, we get stuck.

Why am I resisting my own book? Why, fear of course. Fear of not being able to communicate my vision in a way that readers will connect with. Fear that after I publish, I'll regret not doing a better job. I've been writing this book for eighteen months. It's a part of my life. I do it almost every day. And, mostly, I've loved every moment of it. But soon, I'll have to put my creation out into the world. And the voice that whispers in my head says, "What if no one cares?"

Ugh. It's a wonder any of us ever try anything.

So, what can I do about this Resistance I'm feeling? I have no choice but to turn into it, face it head on, and say *Yes*. And if you, a perfect stranger, are reading this, then you will know that's just what I did.[63]

Say Yes to Imperfection

Our commitment to Yes means changing our relationship with success and failure. This is tough stuff for perfectionists, and most of us experience at least the occasional twinge of perfectionism in our lives. First and

---

[63] By the way, if you've not read Steven Pressfield's *The War of Art*, put this book down and run to the nearest book store to buy a copy. You can thank me later.

foremost, we must accept that we are not our successes and failures. However, both are an opportunity to learn.

Unstuck Project interviewee Andy is the CEO of a rapidly growing international retailer. I see him and his company in the news at least once a week these days. It wasn't always so awesome for Andy. He's fallen down many times. But he hasn't let those times define him. "We've all had failures," he told me. "I'm very good at embracing when things don't go well. I'm not going to be too hard on myself. Nor am I going to think I was the sole cause of what went wrong. Sometimes life just doesn't go your way."

Andy believes that when we fail, we have only one job to do. Get up. And that's a lot easier to do when we're not telling ourselves that we're losers. "People stop," he told me. "That pause is what precludes them from awesome opportunities. I'm faced with failure and disappointment every day. But if I got stuck on everything that didn't go my way, I wouldn't be able to manage. You can't lose sight of the opportunities."

Oh, and when we succeed, same thing goes. Success can mess us up more than failure, especially if we take that success personally. By that, I mean if we put every success down to our own innate talent and we believe that we're successful because we're the *kind of person* who is successful. It may seem counterintuitive, but when we identify with being a successful person, as a lot of perfectionists do, we're a lot less likely to take new risks and learn new things.

Why? Because what if we fail? Who are we then?

Mindset expert Carol Dweck tells us that the strange thing about perfectionism is that it leads us to believe that effort – the one thing absolutely required to achieve our highest potential – is a bad thing.[64] This is obviously terrible thinking, but to the perfectionist, there's a logic to it. If we're naturally smart and talented, everything should come easily. If we have to work at it, then we're not smart and talented; we're stupid and untalented.

Our fear of being perceived as stupid and untalented makes us less likely to seek feedback, because that feedback might be negative. And if it is, it's not only because our performance was less than optimal, it's because we are a bad person. This leaves us ill equipped to address our shortcomings.

Perfectionists are also less likely to give themselves the time required to develop the expertise they need to reach their highest potential. They become easily frustrated and throw in the towel long before those who are willing and able to accept their imperfections and go through the growth and learning required to reach their goals.

To the perfectionist, growth isn't fun, it's painful. It's fraught with landmines. If we fail, we're a failure. If we succeed, the fear of future failure isn't abated, it intensifies.

Perfectionism is a symptom of living in a contractive state. We forget who we really are, prioritize the values about who and how we should be over who and how we could be, and in doing so, we betray ourselves. And we do this, because we think it's the surest way to certainty, significance and love. The problem is, to get those things, we're sacrificing our personal growth and our ability to contribute to the world around us. We become insular and ineffective.

---

[64] Carol S. Dweck, *Mindset, The New Psychology of Success*, Balentine Books, 2006

The imperfect, watery world of Unstuck Leaders such as Andy is by far, the better place to be. Because in that world, we're expansive. In that world, we experiment, fail, succeed and fail some more, all the while inching closer and closer to becoming our best selves.

And this allows us to march, chin up into the emerging future.

EXERCISE

Think about a regret you have that still haunts you. It could be a mistake you made, words you wish you could take back, or a path you wish you had or had not taken.

What did you learn from it?

Were you doing the best you could at the time?

What was your intention?

Have you spoken to others about your regret? Why or why not?

If yes, what was their reaction?

What affect did the action that led to the regret have?

Have you fixed the issues?

If you haven't, or were unable to fix the issues, what did you do to mitigate them?

If someone else had that regret, what would you say to them?

Have you already forgiven someone for something similar?

Would you be able to forgive them? Why?

How would it feel to forgive yourself?

Will you forgive yourself?

After all, when you know better, you do better.

Say Yes to Saying No

Sometimes saying yes to ourselves, means saying no to others. It's all about boundaries. For all our talk about work-life balance, most of us suck at setting boundaries. And that's a real shame, because boundaries are critical to living up to our full potential.

When we fail to establish tight boundaries, we keep ourselves small. If we say yes when we really should say no, it's because we're operating from a place of fear. When we give in to our fears, we slip into a contractive state.

Saying no in the right circumstances keeps us grounded. When we're clear about what we will and won't do, we earn the respect of others. And we gain some self-respect as well, which frees us to live our values and fulfill our true purpose for our lives.

And this puts us in an expansive state.

Now we're playing big.

Sounds simple enough, but it's not always that easy.

I had a client, we'll call her Lisa, who headed up customer success at a fast-growing company. Already, there's ripe potential for boundary issues as by its very nature, customer success requires us to put the customer first. And, in Lisa's case, this service mentality spilled into all areas of her life.

When she first came to me, she wanted to grow a bigger voice for herself around the office. And she wanted her team to get the respect she felt they deserved. Customer success may not bring revenue in the door, but it certainly keeps it from leaving by turning angry customers into happy ones.

As Lisa's company grew, so did her team, though perhaps not fast enough. It seemed there was never enough time in the day to answer all the customer issues, hire new employees, set policies, write manuals and train team members. On top of her day-to-day duties, Lisa was booked into back-to-back meetings, leaving her unable to get any of her real work done during the day.

So, rather than rock the boat and say no to the meetings, Lisa wrote to-do lists of all the work she would do at night. She'd go home, make dinner and hang out with her two children, clean up, throw in a load of laundry and then she would get to work. Usually the work started around

10PM. And she'd finish around 2AM. Every weekday. Weekends weren't much better. Lisa was afraid to ask her boss for a weekend staff member to help her out because she didn't want her boss to know that she couldn't handle everything on her own.

At the same time, Lisa knew this life was unsustainable. I actually don't know how she was able to do it for as long as she was. It's actually very impressive. But her work was suffering. She wasn't able to think strategically, because she was exhausted. She was living off five hours of sleep per night. When her colleagues started joking about receiving emails from her at 2AM, she began setting them so they would send at 9AM instead. She didn't want anyone to know how hard she was working.

The moment she told me that, when she heard herself say that she was hiding her hard work from her colleagues, was the moment a light bulb went on for Lisa.

Her department wasn't respected, because she was too afraid to tell everyone how hard they worked. She said yes to each and every meeting, because she worried she'd be seen as uncooperative by her colleagues. She didn't delegate to her employees, because she didn't want to put extra pressure on them. She didn't ask her boss for more resources, because she was raised not to complain and not to demand things (often the boundaries we do or don't set are the result of subtle or not-so-subtle messages we receive as children).

Lisa finally committed to setting boundaries. So, we got to work. And Lisa learned to say no so she could say yes to herself.

Boundary 1: How we spend our time

As it was in Lisa's case, usually the boundaries that need to be set most urgently are those around how we spend our time. Time to do our best work, time with our partner, family and friends, time to be creative, go to the gym, make a good dinner, etc.

We all know that we should treat time as our most precious resource, but few of us actually take that notion seriously. Ironically, the only time I notice the fleeting nature of time is when I've been in a flow state and realize I've lost several hours while deep in focus on something important to me. Other times, when I'm bored or feeling sorry for myself, time crawls to a near standstill and I have to remind myself that it's all an illusion. It's quite the paradox really, but look, I don't make the rules. All I know is once it's gone, it never comes back. So, we might as well spend it as well as we can.

When feeling overwhelmed, Amelia, a Tech CEO, tells her staff that she needs an "introverted day". She works from home, goes for a walk, and does what's needed to recharge. And by the next day, she's ready to tackle the world again.

Good for Amelia. Researchers from Duke university have discovered that silence aids in the increased development of new neurons – specifically those located in the hippocampus which is the part of our brains associated with learning.[65]

---

[65] Kirste, Imke & Nicola, Zeina & Kronenberg, Golo & Walker, Tara & Liu, Robert & Kempermann, Gerd. (2013). "Is silence golden? Effects of auditory stimuli and their absence on adult hippocampal neurogenesis." *Brain structure & function.* 10.1007/s00429-013-0679-3.

Tracy and Don, partners and co-founders of a tech startup they run out of their home have made the room where they work (the dining room) off limits in the evenings and on weekends. This prevents them from working around the clock and gives them time to reconnect with themselves and with each other.

Boundary 2: Whom we let into our lives

It's an unfortunate fact that not everyone in the world is a happy ray of sunshine. There are in fact, quite a few negative people. And they can drain our energy. We must think carefully about how often we let them into our lives.

For those people who are negative, but who matter to you and you want to keep in your life, it's all about communication. Tell them how their behavior is affecting you. Ask for what you need. Teach them how to give it to you.

For those who don't matter, it's a little easier. As writer Wes Moore says, "Don't let people who don't matter too much, matter too much." Wise words. You don't actually have to have negative people in your life. And if they are in your life because they're a co-worker, or just someone who's going to be around, you don't have to let them matter too much.

Am I saying you need to eliminate anyone suffering from depression or anxiety from your life? Absolutely not. If they matter to you, and you want to support them, do so. But, be aware of the effect they have on your energy and take time to care and replenish yourself before and after contact with them. You're no good to anyone if you allow yourself to become depleted.

Boundary 3: Where we direct our attention

I've said it before, and I'll say it again: Where focus goes, energy flows. Are you going to focus on the negativity of the office gossip to day? Or on doing a great job on your latest project? On the stinging pain of that recent failure, or on the success of the next big thing? On that other guy's success, or on creating your own?

Included in this is what we read and watch. We have a device in our pocket (that would be our phones) that has been designed to make us look at it constantly in search of the tiny dopamine hit our brains get from something new. If you're finding you're having difficulty controlling your screen time, consider setting personal boundaries about when you look by using a screen time monitor app.

Setting these three simple boundaries will free you to do your best work. When we're clear about what we will and won't do, we're on firm ground. And, because of this, people will respect our boundaries. Over time, there's less need to enforce them and that means we don't have to say no as often.

But for the times we do have to say no, take the advice of TV producer Shonda Rhimes. She simply says, "I'm sorry, no, I'm not able to do that."

It's clear, it's forthright and it's really hard to argue with.

EXERCISE:

Think of an area in your life where you're playing small (saying yes to others) rather than big (saying yes to yourself).

When you think about that part of your life, what fears are coming into play?

Think of a boundary you could set that would enable you to play big.

What would a tighter boundary look like? How would you make it work?

Say Yes to Connection

It shouldn't be lonely at the top. So if it is, we need to do a rethink, because for Unstuck Leaders, connection, both within our organization and outside of it is imperative.

If our teams feel connected to us and each other, trust will grow. And trust is vital to co-creation. Without trust, we would find it impossible to ride the waves of uncertainty, ambiguity and risk that result from well-functioning complex adaptive systems. We would find it impossible to be expansive. And we would become stuck.

In her book, *Dare to Lead*, Brené Brown writes that "It turns out, that trust is in fact earned in the smallest of moments. It is earned not through heroic deeds or even highly visible actions, but through paying attention, listening, and gestures of genuine care and connection."

That last bit is important – the connection must be "genuine". We can't fake connection. We can't say we're interested in our colleagues only to glaze over when they attempt to tell us about something that's important to them. We can't say we care about work-life balance and then expect our team members to be online 24/7.

Genuine connection that leads to trust requires us to acknowledge the good stuff and the tough stuff. It requires us to admit when something isn't working. It requires us to confess when we have doubt. It requires us to recognize excellent performance, as well as to notice the small, quiet things that lead to big results. It requires us to see strength and talent and differences and to encourage and enable and accommodate. It requires us to forgive, and to have faith.

Well-connected teams are bonded by a common language and shared purpose. Their connection is expressed in kindness and mutual regard. They laugh a lot, are incredibly resilient and are able to overcome seemingly insurmountable obstacles. They are exactly the type of team we all hope to be a part of.

Unstuck Leaders are also connected to a large network of people outside of their organization. This exposes them to new ideas, emerging trends and previously unseen possibilities. And from this exposure, a new sense of confidence grows.

J. Kelly Hoey, author of *Build Your Dream Network* says that, "When you know people and those people know what you do, success knows how to find you."

Building a great network begins with curiosity and generosity. It does not necessarily begin with schmoozing at a networking event, so if the idea of saddling up to a stranger while holding a cocktail fills you with dread, have no fear. Networking is really about being useful to people. And in time, they will choose to be useful to you too.

We meet people all the time – customers, suppliers, contractors, etc. Get curious about them. Ask about their job, their company, their industry, their challenges and interests. And then, when you come across an opportunity or piece of information that may be useful to them, send it their way. Over time, you may connect with them on social media, meet them for a coffee or a lunch, and bam, before you know it, you have a meaningful relationship.

And the rewards of this relationship are enormous. Your network will connect you to more people with whom you can create other meaningful relationships. They will come to you with ideas and opportunities, draw your attention to organizations and occurrences that may have slipped your notice and invite you to events where learning may happen and additional connections may be made.

Over time, if you get really good at networking, you may decide to become the kind of person who connects people to other people. Unstuck Project interviewee Jack, who has been a successful CEO from the age of 23, found himself adrift at the age of 32. He was no longer certain that the company he built and the industry he built it in were where he wanted to be. So, to sort through his feelings, Jack turned to mindfulness meditation. Not only did the meditation help him come to a greater appreciation of the company he'd created, it helped him arrive at a new purpose in his life – to share the benefit and value of mindfulness in the business community. He began inviting small groups of entrepreneurs and business leaders to evening discussions about mindfulness. The participants in those early groups introduced Jack to other business leaders who were interested in mindfulness. Soon, the evening discussions spread to other cities. By expanding his attention beyond himself, Jack not only grew into a new purpose, but he also became a connector. And now he has a huge network of like-minded business people. His world is bigger, and so are his possibilities.

Unstuck Project interviewee Elias has created a network of business leaders who meet for five hours once a month to help each other work through issues and to make tough decisions. In other words, they help each other get and stay unstuck. In his words, "We air it, think about it and work on it. We hear what everyone in the group has to say. We call it sharing. We communicate in a way that a person can receive it. The idea is to help the entrepreneur deal with what it means to be an entrepreneur. That is, uncertainty and absurdity."

Elias has been hosting these meetings for 25 years. And he's one of the least stuck people I interviewed.

At its core, connection is about showing up – showing up for your employees, showing up for your colleagues and bosses, and showing up for those in your network. It takes time. It takes kindness and understanding.

And it takes commitment.

Say Yes to Commitment

Commitment is an act, not a word.

– Jean-Paul Sartre

Paul, an Unstuck Project interviewee worked for years as a senior executive at a huge telecommunications company – exactly the kind of bureaucratic nightmare of a place where even the best-intentioned employees find themselves frustrated, stymied, a little bitter and a lot stuck. And eventually, they would find their way into Paul's office. Paul was known for mentoring younger colleagues.

"This is how I see the universe," he told me. "When someone comes to me with a problem, I get excited for them. I smile and say, 'That's great!'."

You see, Paul loves stuckness. He seeks it out. Because to him, stuckness doesn't mean he's done something wrong, it means something is waiting to happen. And when someone declares their stuckness to someone else, they make the thing that wants to happen that much closer to reality.

"I've been stuck at least 30 times," Paul told me. "I choose to be stuck. I look for stuckness. To me, it's obvious. Pick anything. It's easy to choose to do something. But then you have to do it." Then, he laughed at me. "You did a brilliant thing. You announced publicly that you're going to write this book. The moment you did that, you did the trick. You made yourself stuck. Now you have to do it."

He was right.

That's commitment.

Without commitment, our leadership practice isn't a practice at all. It's a dilly-dally; a thing we're trying on for a while. Without commitment, our leadership lacks authenticity. In short, without commitment, we're all talk and no action. And that's the very definition of stuck.

Commitment means daily practice. It's easy to read this book, and perhaps think some of the ideas in it are good ones, and maybe even to try a few of them out. But if you forget them the minute the next crisis comes along, you'll have wasted time and psychic energy for nothing. If you know what to do, and then don't do it, it's worse than never having read the book at all.

Continued daily practice means ritual. It's up to us to create the circumstances in which we are most likely to commit to upholding our values, fulfilling our purpose and to focusing on growth and contribution. For some of us, it's mindfulness, in the form of meditation, or yoga, or cooking, or running, or knitting, or whatever it is that quiets our minds and propels us to a singular focus. For others, it's a morning routine. For others it's visualization.

Writer and entrepreneur James Altucher realized that there are four things that if done consistently, help him weather any storm, up to and including losing several million dollars in a single day.[66] With this knowledge, he

---

[66] Watch Altucher's terrific interview with Chase Jarvis where he explains both that multi-million-dollar loss, and also the check-box system that helped him weather the storm: https://youtu.be/1qLBFOkk-0A

created a check-box system. Each day, he just checks the boxes:

1. Am I doing something for my physical health?

2. Am I doing something for my personal relationships?

3. Am I doing something creative?

4. Am I practicing gratitude?

Just doing those four simple things every day has given James exceptional resilience. And if an Unstuck Leader is anything, it's resilient.

I have a system not unlike James's four simple things. I like to remind myself of four simple truths.

I remind myself that I am brave. I start with that one because as Maya Angelou said, "Courage is the most important of all the virtues, because it allows you to practice the others with consistency."[67]

I remind myself that I am grateful. For my husband, my family, my friends, my clients, and my Unstuck Project interviewees; as well as the times when the street car turns up just as I get to the stop.

I remind myself that I am kind. Not nice. Nice is superficial. I mean genuinely kind.

And, I remind myself that I'm doing my best. And I am.

---

[67] Angelou says this while being interviewed by Dave Chappelle. Watch it here: https://youtu.be/okc6COsgzoE you won't regret it. They're both incredible.

For me, these four simple truths are profoundly powerful. Because if I commit to practicing them daily, the rest, I can leave up to the universe. And so, I do.[68]

---

[68] And if all else fails, I listen to *This Girl is on Fire* by Alicia Keys.

A Final Word

I can't quite quit you yet. There's one last thing I need to tell you. Here it is: Your career will most certainly not go to plan.

You'll be denied that promotion you deserve. Or maybe your new boss will turn out to be a jerk, or a spineless wimp, or a bit of a dumb-dumb. Or maybe you'll be saddled with a project you don't want. Or maybe you'll have a health crisis that will keep you out of the game for a spell.

None of it will be your fault. But the consequences will be yours to live with.

Ten years ago, I sat in a meeting with two of my bosses (I actually had three at the time), as they told me that a product I built and launched and grew to profitability was being moved to another division of the company. When I objected (because I believed the other division would screw up the product – and they did), I was told that my attitude was unacceptable and that I needed to be more of a team player.

The entire situation was bullshit.

The organization had been in utter chaos for some time. Those two bosses were playing at corporate politics, and losing, and so they were throwing me under the bus. And we all knew it.

At first, I was angry about the unfairness of it all, but then, right there in the meeting, something amazing happened. It was as if someone had flipped a switch in my head. I swear I actually heard the click.

I realized: I don't have to work here anymore.

And suddenly, I was in charge. I told them I understood and left the room. The next day, I began networking. And six months later, when I walked out the door with a package, I had options. Lots of them.

Unstuck Project interviewee Emma had a similar experience. She was stressed and overwhelmed in a thankless job. "I was traveling for work, staying at a dodgy motel across the street from a Chuck E. Cheese and I finally thought, *What the hell am I doing*?" She quit her job shortly after and now she's the CEO of another organization.

Like me, Unstuck Project interviewee Sophia had her ah-ha moment in a meeting. "Business was really hard. We spent more time pointing fingers and making excuses than accomplishing anything. I realized; this isn't going to get better." She called an ex-boss immediately after the meeting and was in a new job two weeks later.

Unstuck Project interviewee Sawyer's decision to move on came slowly, but after years of feeling stuck, he finally did it. "The decision to leave was hard. I had a young family and I didn't know where I would go. But I thought I'd rather take control. It was cathartic and liberating." He's the president of another company now.

You are not powerless. This is your life and your career. You're in charge of your experience. You're in charge of what you take from it and what you give to it. But mostly, you're in charge of how you respond to its challenges.

Sometimes, being in charge means letting go and moving on, as it was for me, Emma, Sophia and Sawyer. And sometimes, being in charge means digging deeper and making the most of what you have, where you are.

It's about asking yourself: What can I make of this?

You may have had a project blow up in your face, but you learned a ton from it. Or, your financial situation may make it unwise to quit right now, but the experience you're gaining will make you highly marketable in a year or two. It could be that your jerk/spineless/dumb-dumb boss is helping to hone your communication and influence skills.

Maybe, just maybe, there's a hint of possibility, even in the darkness. And before you tell me that your situation is particularly impossible, let me tell you about an architect named Chris Downey.

At the age of 45, a brain tumor left Chris completely blind. It's usually best if architects aren't blind, but this didn't stop Chris. He never thought his sight loss was insurmountable. Rather, he realized that the creative process of architecture isn't so much about what you can see, but how you think.

So, a month after he went blind, he went back to work. He has a special printer that creates raised lines enabling him to feel blueprints. And, he uses bendy wax sticks to design and modify the drawings.

And he discovered something really cool about being blind. He can no longer see buildings, but he can hear their acoustics and feel their textures. This new perspective has made him a truly unique architect. And, a better architect. "It's not about what I'm missing in architecture," he said. "It's about what I *had* been missing in architecture."

It wasn't easy. Chris sees nothing. No shadow, no light, nothing. He's in total darkness.

His story reminds me of an essay by Valarie Kaur that a lovely and thoughtful client forwarded to me recently. It has a beautiful line in it: "What if this darkness is not the darkness of the tomb, but the darkness of the womb?"[69]

In other words, what if the loss of Chris's sight, or the loss of a product, or a promotion or a job, isn't about the death of something, but rather, about something new wanting to be born?

Chris now specializes in making spaces accessible to the blind. He's worked on a rehabilitation center for veterans with sight loss, as well as spaces at Duke University Hospital, Microsoft and the San Francisco Transit Center.

He does what no other architect can do. And he has his answer to the question: What can I make of this?

"I took my disability and turned it upside down," he says.[70] And of that, a new kind of architect was born.

So let me ask: What inside of you is wanting to be born?

You don't have to wait for tragedy, pain and suffering to jolt you into action. Too often we wait for things to be born of necessity. But what if they could be born of love?

Why not? After all, you're in charge.

Got it? Good. Now go get 'em.

---

[69] ValarieKaur.com, "A Sikh Prayer for America on November 9th, 2016".

[70] You can watch Chris's appearance on 60 Minutes here. Fair warning: you'll want to have some hankies nearby. https://www.cbsnews.com/video/architect-chris-downey-goes-blind-says-hes-actually-gotten-better-at-his-job-60-minutes/

ACKNOWLEDGEMENTS

To the Unstuck Project Interviewees

You shared with me your moments of greatest heartbreak, pain and triumph. You confessed your deepest fears. Sometimes you were funny and wry. Sometimes you were raw and hurting. Always, you were honest and thoughtful. You inspired me. You made me better at what I do. This book could not exist without you. I am overwhelmed by your generosity, and I thank you.

To my Sister Women

Iyanla Vanzant once said that when we are most in need, a "sister-woman" will appear to help us. Though you may not know it, Nancy Peterson and Karen Mazurkewich, you were those sister women for me. At a time when I needed it most, you each called upon me to be at my best. Thank you for your faith and kindness.

To Cindy Sims and Paul Sims

On a June day when I was eight years old and you were just fourteen and sixteen, you came and took me out of school in the middle of the afternoon. You told my teacher that I had a dental appointment, and I believed you until I saw that Paul's old yellow van was loaded with a half dozen of your friends.

I'd been begging you to let me come along on one of your school-skipping afternoons. And at last, you did, on the condition that I never tell our mother.

We went to a swimming hole. We floated in inner tubes on sparkling water. There was the smell of Hawaiian Tropic dark tanning oil and the taste of warm root beer. I remember lying in the grass, looking up at the glorious Alberta blue sky and feeling so happy.

In my memory, that afternoon was bathed in sunlight. And so were the two of you. You were golden.

You taught me how to break the rules that day.

And I'll always be grateful.

And most importantly, to John Ferri

You are the love of my life, the best thing on two legs and the bee's knees. Your dedication to making the world better for those at the bottom, and uncomfortable for those at the top has inspired me again and again. Your faith in me has been astounding, as is your ability to catch me when I fall. You're also very good at *Jeopardy*.

I'm a lucky woman.

Index

About the Author

Judy Sims is a writer, strategy consultant and Board Certified Coach™. She helps leaders get and stay unstuck so they can thrive in a world that is growing more complex, more challenging, and less predictable. Previously, she was a co-founder and CEO of tech start-up Shopcaster, Vice President of Digital Media at the *Toronto Star* and Founding Publisher of the magazine *Weekly Scoop*. Her mission is to change the world, one Unstuck Leader at a time.

You can learn more about Judy and apply to become a consulting or coaching client at https://judysims.com.

Made in the USA
Middletown, DE
25 July 2019